Musician's Guide to Copyright

Musician's GUIDE TO COPYRIGHT

REVISED EDITION

J. Gunnar Erickson Edward R. Hearn
Mark E. Halloran
bay area lawyers for the arts

CHARLES SCRIBNER'S SONS · NEW YORK

Library of Congress Cataloging in Publication Data

Erickson, J. Gunnar, 1946–
Musician's guide to copyright.

Includes bibliographical references and index.
1. Copyright—Music—United States. 2. Copyright—Sound recordings—United States. I. Hearn, Edward R. II. Halloran, Mark E. III. Title.
KF3035.E74 1983 346.7304'82 83–3295
ISBN 0–684–17900–8 347.306482

This book published simultaneously in the United States of America and in Canada—Copyright under the Berne Convention.

1 3 5 7 9 11 13 15 17 19 F/C 20 18 16 14 12 10 8 6 4 2

Printed in the United States of America.

Contents

bay area lawyers for the arts

BALA was conceived by a group of artists and lawyers in August 1974 to meet the legal needs of artists and arts organizations in the San Francisco Bay Area. It is modeled on legal assistance organizations such as Volunteer Lawyers for the Arts (VLA) in New York City, which was founded in 1969, and similar organizations that are now active in Boston, Chicago, Portland, and elsewhere.

BALA's primary function is to provide legal assistance; to this end the organization has established a panel of some 200 volunteer attorneys who are willing to help eligible artists (including musicians) and arts organizations on any art-related legal problem. Such problems include questions of copyright, contract, libel, tax, and nonprofit incorporation—to name a few—in the visual, performing, and literary arts. Any Bay Area artist or arts organization may call BALA for assistance.

Other activities include providing legal rights education programs for artists; training attorneys in arts law, which is a rapidly changing and expanding field; and preparing publications that deal with general areas of the legal aspects of art.

Acknowledgments

The authors and BALA would like to express their gratitude to a number of people who provided valuable advice and assistance during the preparation of the original edition. We owe a particular debt to: Michael Ashburne, whose helpful commentary on early drafts of the work made the rewrites more effective; to Marilyn Mason, for typing draft after draft of the manuscript; and to Robert Krimmer, a dedicated law student from Hastings School of Law, who invested a substantial amount of his very limited time in checking references and cleaning up notes so that this book could be a valuable tool for the practicing lawyer as well as the practicing artist. Thanks are also due to Scott Riklin, who edited and supervised the production of the text; as well as Juan Fuentes, who created the cover and book design of the first edition. A special debt of gratitude is owed to Barbara Kibbe for her tireless and generous efforts in getting the book published.

Naturally, the legal opinions included in this publication are those of the authors and not necessarily those of the other contributors nor of Bay Area Lawyers for the Arts.

Introduction

This guide to music copyrights is written to give songwriters, musicians, managers and attorneys a working knowledge of U.S. copyright law. The Copyright Revision Act of 1976, which went into effect on January 1, 1978, changed copyright law and introduced an entirely new set of copyright forms. This book explains those changes and the use of the new forms.

Copyright is a complicated field of law, and although we have made an effort to be straightforward in our explanation of the copyright law, we did not simplify when that risked losing significant details. Matters mainly of interest to lawyers are placed in the notes at the end of the volume. Even so, we do not expect each person who uses this book to read it from cover to cover. The Contents, therefore, is detailed to help each reader focus on specific questions that he or she may need to review.

Although this book should be useful in giving an overall view of music copyright law, we urge you to seek the advice of a music attorney to help you with specific legal problems relating to music.

Musician's Guide to Copyright

Fundamentals of Copyright Law in the United States

CHAPTER
ONE

BACKGROUND

Copyright in the United States is founded on a provision of the U.S. Constitution that authorizes Congress to enact laws to give authors exclusive rights in their writings for limited times.[1] Over the years that constitutional provision has been implemented by Congress through various statutes[2] and regulations.[3] In 1976, the copyright law in the United States was changed by the Copyright Revision Act of 1976, which went into effect on January 1, 1978.[4]

The Copyright Act has counterparts in most other countries and is tied to its foreign counterparts by international treaties that combine to produce, in effect, a network of world copyright laws.[5] The foundation of this body of copyright law is an English statute enacted in the early eighteenth century. At that time, the invention of the printing press made it possible for increasing numbers of people to obtain books and other works of art. There were no legal means, however, to prevent one person from taking another's book, engraving, or other work and reproducing it for sale. As a result, the creator often lost all commercial benefit (and sometimes all recognition) from the work. In response, the English Parliament enacted the English Copyright Act of 1709.[6] That Act and later legislation gave the creator of a work the exclusive right to reproduce the work and to enjoy the economic benefit of that reproduction. This was the first time that English law recognized as an independent right the commercial benefit that a creator of a work of art should enjoy as a result of creating the work. The method chosen for granting artists and writers this protection was to grant them rights, defined by the statute, and to use the court system for enforcing the rights. Copyright, then, is a *property* right and its extent and limits are those defined by the law. Originally, the right was in fact a *copy right*, the exclusive right to make copies.

Over the past two and a half centuries the scope of materials subject to copyright protection and the nature of that protection have been widened greatly. The large array of artistic works presently entitled to copyright protection includes musical compositions, books, magazines, songs, pantomimes, choreographic works, paintings, sculptures, murals, motion pictures, advertising material, fabric designs, and sound recordings.

WHAT CAN BE COPYRIGHTED

To qualify for copyright protection under the Copyright Act a work must be original to the author and must be fixed in a tangible medium of expression.[7] To understand this statement and what copyright means, it is important to grasp the legal meaning of the following terms:

ORIGINAL. To be *original* under the Copyright Act a work need not pass any requirement of novelty, ingenuity, or aesthetic merit. That a work is original means nothing more than that the work is original to the author; that is, he or she made the work.[8] Conceivably the same or a similar work could be created by someone else. As long as those same or similar works are created by their respective authors *independently* of one another, each work is entitled to copyright protection.

FIXED. A work of art is considered to be *fixed* when it has been put in a tangible medium of expression (for example, on paper or on tape) so that it can be perceived, reproduced, or otherwise communicated for a period of more than transitory duration.[9] Having an idea for a song and singing the song to a friend or to an audience does not constitute a fixing; if the song is recorded or transcribed, however, then it has become sufficiently fixed in a tangible medium of expression to qualify for copyright protection.

CREATED. At the time the work of art is fixed, it is considered to have been *created* and as of that moment is entitled to protection under the Copyright Act.[10]

PUBLICATION. *Publication* is the distribution of copies of a work of art or phonorecords of a sound recording to the public by sale or some other means of transferring ownership or control over the work, such as renting, leasing, lending, or even giving the work away.[11] Consequently, distributing copies or phonorecords to a group of persons for the purpose of public distribution, public performance, or public display by them would constitute a publication. A public performance of a work (for example, the acting out of a pantomime or the singing of a song)[12] does not constitute a publication since there has been no transfer of ownership resulting from that performance.[13] Sending a demo record of a song to a publisher or record company for review generally is not a publication when the demo is only for the recipient to listen to and there is no intent that the demo be publicly distributed.

WORKS. *Works* are the creations of authors that the Copyright Act protects. The Act divides works into seven broad categories:

1. literary works
2. musical works (including accompanying words)
3. dramatic works (including accompanying music)
4. pantomimes and choreographic works

5. pictorial, graphic, and sculptural works
6. motion pictures and other audiovisual works
7. sound recordings.[14]

It should be noted that these categories sometimes overlap and are not exclusive. In the musical field, the most important works are musical works and sound recordings.

MUSICAL WORKS. The most familiar example of a *musical work* is a song—both lyrics and music together comprise the work. Symphonies and other musical creations that can be performed are also musical works.[15] Contracts usually refer to a song as a "musical composition."

SOUND RECORDING. A *sound recording* is a work that is a series of recorded sounds.[16] For example, the performance of a song on a tape constitutes a sound recording. It is important to remember that the sound recording and the song itself are separate, independent *works*. Each time an artist records "White Christmas" a separate sound recording or work is created. The song "White Christmas" itself, however, is a single musical work separate and apart from the individual sound recordings made by others. To run that by once again: a song is a musical work, and each sound recording of that song is a separate work in its own right.

COPY. A *copy* is not a work; it is the physical manifestation of the work.[17] In general, a copy is an object from which a work can be *visually* perceived. Lead sheets and other notated music are copies of a musical work.

PHONORECORD. A *phonorecord* is not a work; rather, it is a physical object, typically audiotapes and phonograph records, embodying the fixed sounds of a sound recording.[18] A phonorecord is *not* a *copy* of a sound recording, because the audio performance is not directly represented in a visual form.

Musical works and sound recordings therefore are published in the form of copies and phonorecords, respectively. When a copy of sheet music is sold, the songs in it are published. When a phonorecord is sold, the sound recording is published, and under the 1976 Copyright Act, so is the song (musical work) on the phonorecord.

WHAT CANNOT BE COPYRIGHTED

We also should point out that copyright does not protect the ideas or concepts contained in a work.[19] Copyright merely protects the form of expression. For example, the rock group The Who could not copyright the concept of a rock opera even if they originated the idea. The group could copyright the songs comprising *Tommy* and its sound recording of the songs, but anyone else could compose his or her own rock opera.

The names of songs cannot be protected by a copyright. The Copyright Office takes the position that song titles, as well as other short slogans and phrases, lack sufficient literary content to be copyrighted.[20] You could write a song and call it "John Wesley Harding" and not violate Bob Dylan's copyright to the song of the same name. You could, however, encounter serious legal problems under state statutes if you attempted to pass off your song as Dylan's or marketed the song in a way that confused people about the authorship.

U.S. COPYRIGHT OFFICE

The Copyright Act is administered by the Copyright Office of the Library of Congress in Washington, D.C., under the direction of the Register of Copyrights.[21] The Register issues regulations that are used to put into effect the provisions of the Act.[22] The regulations deal with such issues as registering copyright claims and copyright transfers and depositing copies of the copyrighted work.

During the year 1981, the Copyright Office handled over one million pieces of mail and processed more than 600,000 copyright registrations. The Copyright Office examines the submitted registration forms in each of the eligible classifications, registers those that meet the requirements of the Act, and catalogs the registration. If the submitted work is not eligible for registration or the form has not been completed correctly, the Copyright Office will reject the registration, returning it to the sender. Under the Act, the Copyright Office may keep the submitted copies of the work even though the claim has been rejected.[23]

The Copyright Office does not offer legal advice on copyright law, but does answer questions about the methods of securing copyright and the procedures for registration. (For more about registration, see chapter 2.)

The records of the Copyright Office are open for public inspection. Upon payment of a fee, anyone can obtain a report from the Copyright Office concerning any particular deposit, registration, or recorded document.[24] Also, copies of the Copyright Office's public records or indexes and additional certificates of copyright registrations can be obtained on request for a fee.[25]

The Copyright Office periodically compiles and publishes catalogs of all copyright registrations and furnishes at no charge copyright registration forms and general information material.[26] (See "Registering Songs" in chapter 2 for a discussion of those forms relevant to musicians.) To obtain copyright registration forms or answers to questions concerning copyright notices and registrations, you can write to the Copyright Office at the Library of Congress, Washington, D.C. 20559 or call the Copyright Office at (202) 287–9100.

PUBLIC DOMAIN

Copyrights do not last forever. The Constitution empowered Congress to protect an author's writing "for limited times." Thus, under the old law, the term of copyright could not exceed fifty-six years, and under the new law the general term is the life of the author plus fifty years. (For a discussion of the duration period of copyright, see chapter 3.) If no copyright is claimed, no copyright exists: you are free to use the work of authorship without any restrictions. For example, if someone writes a song and wishes to dedicate the song to the public, the song would be published without a copyright notice and would fall into the public domain.

A more typical situation is that in which a copyright has expired. If you want to use a copyrighted work when the term of copyright may have expired, you can write the Copyright Office for the copyright status of the work.[27] If the copyright term has expired, the work falls into the *public domain;* in other words, the work belongs to the public, not an individual copyright proprietor. You are free to use public domain work in any way you want, at least in the United States.

OWNERSHIP

Under the Copyright Act a copyright in a work belongs to the person who created it,[28] and only the owner of a copyright or his or her agent can file an application to register the copyright with the Register of Copyrights.[29] When more than one person is involved in creating the work, there are some variations on this theme.

A *collective work* is a work combining several independently copyrighted works.[30] With collective works, the copyright in a contribution belongs to the author of that contribution and is distinct from a copyright in the collective work as a whole.[31] For example, if a song book were published containing the songs of Joan Baez, Tom Rush, and Phil Ochs, the copyright owners of the individual songs would continue to own those copyrights. Also, there would be a separate copyright available in the book that joined each of those songs in the collective work.[32] We should point out that the person responsible for putting the songs together in the collective work must have permission from the copyright owners of the individual songs before the collective work is published. Otherwise, the publication of the collective work is an infringement of the copyright in the individual songs.

Unless there has been an express written transfer of the copyright in a separate contribution to the owner of the collective work, the owner of the copyright in the collective work will have acquired only the privilege of reproducing and distributing the songs as a part of the collective work and could not print and distribute the songs individually.[33]

A *joint work* differs from a collective work in that contributions to a joint work become part of an inseparable whole, with each of the contributors taking an undivided interest in the whole.[34] A simple illustration of a joint work is the case of two songwriters joining talents to write the music and lyrics for one song—for example, Elton John and Bernie Tarpin co-authoring "Your Song." They would each be co-owners of that song.

There are two kinds of *works made for hire:* (1) those prepared by an employee within the scope of his or her employment, and (2) a specially ordered or commissioned work within prescribed categories, such as a contribution to a collective work (like a motion picture or book) when the parties expressly agree in a signed statement that the work will be considered a work made for hire. If you are employed to write a song, the song will be owned by the employer, the person responsible for hiring the artist to make the work. The employer owns the copyright in the absence of an express, written agreement between the employer and the artist indicating that the arrangement is otherwise.[35] So, if NBC hired Gil Scott-Heron as an employee to write a theme song for a television special, NBC would be the copyright owner of that song, and Scott-Heron would have no rights in the song, unless NBC and Scott-Heron specifically contracted otherwise.

With *specially ordered or commissioned works* for use as a contribution to a collective work, the copyright stays with the artist unless there is a written agreement to the contrary.[36] If George Lucas commissions Leonard Bernstein to write the music for *Star Wars III* and it is clear that Bernstein is not an employee, and the contract does not describe the score as a specially ordered or commissioned work to be done as a work for hire, then Bernstein owns the copyright to that music. The new Act reverses the prior rule that the purchaser, rather than the artist, is entitled to claim the statutory copyright in specially ordered or commissioned works in the absence of a contrary agreement.

As you can see, the distinction between works made for hire and specially ordered or commissioned works not specified in writing as a work for hire is crucial, since that distinction determines the copyright ownership to the work in the absence of a written agreement between the parties directing otherwise. When you are paid to write a song that will be used in a film, in a commercial, or by a performer, make certain that you reach a written understanding on who will own the copyright in the work. If the agreement is silent about ownership, but describes you as an "employee," or describes the song as "made for hire" or a "specially ordered or commissioned work" done as a work for hire, you will not own the copyright.

RIGHTS PROVIDED BY COPYRIGHT

A copyright, as a property right, can be subdivided into separate parts that are individually protected.[37] This concept is referred to as the divisibility of copyright; in effect, a copyright is a "bundle of rights." Under the Copyright Act, each of the parts of a copyright belongs to the copyright owner, and others can use the work only after getting permission from the copyright owner (usually by paying).[38]

The five general rights in the "bundle" include:

1. the right to reproduce the copyrighted work in either copies or phonorecords[39]
2. the right to prepare derivative works based on the copyrighted work[40]
3. the right to distribute to the public copies or phonorecords of the copyrighted work[41]
4. the right to perform publicly a literary, musical, dramatic or choreographic work, pantomime, motion picture, or other audiovisual work[42]
5. the right to display publicly a copyrighted literary, dramatic, musical or choreographic work, a pantomime or pictorial, graphic or sculptural work, including the individual images in a motion picture or other audiovisual work.[43]

As is discussed in chapter 4—which examines the commercial exploitation rights of the copyright owner—each of these five parts can be subdivided further. For example, a copyright owner can license someone to reproduce a work but limit the license in time, quantity, or manner of reproduction.[44]

LIMITATIONS ON EXCLUSIVE RIGHTS

The Copyright Act does impose some limitations on the exclusive rights just discussed. The *fair use* and the *not-for-profit* exemptions are two of these limitations, and they affect the copyright owner's ability to restrict or charge for the use of the copyrighted work.[45]

Under the Copyright Act, the doctrine of *fair use* authorizes the use of a copyrighted work for purposes such as criticism, comment, news reporting, teaching, scholarship, or research.[46] Generally, the use must be limited and not affect the market for or impair the commercial value of the copyrighted work.

The Act identifies four factors to be applied in determining whether a use is a fair use. These factors include:

1. the purpose and character of the use (including whether the use is of a commercial nature or for non-profit educational purposes)
2. the nature of the copyrighted work itself
3. the amount and substantiality of the portion of the copyrighted work used
4. the effect of the use on the commercial value of the copyrighted work.[47]

In the abstract, these four factors do little to explain or show when a fair use can be claimed. The meaning of these four factors is determined by their application in each fact situation that may arise. For example, a teacher copying the lyrics from a Bob Dylan song to use in a literary course on the poetry of contemporary music could argue that this use is fair. But if the teacher made multiple copies of many lyrics to avoid buying sheet music, a persuasive argument could be made that such use is not a fair use.[48]

A second limitation on the exclusive rights of the copyright owner is the *not-for-profit* exemption, which allows the use of a copyrighted work in certain non-commercial circumstances.[49] The allowed uses include certain educational, religious, charitable, and governmental functions.[50]

COMPULSORY MECHANICAL LICENSES AS A LIMITATION ON EXCLUSIVE RIGHTS IN MUSICAL WORKS

The fair use and not-for-profit limitations[51] on a copyright owner's rights apply to all types of works. There is also a special provision in the Copyright Act that further limits rights in recorded musical works. Of the five general rights associated with copyright (see "Rights Provided by Copyright" above), two—the right to reproduce the copyrighted work in phonorecords (1) and the right to publicly distribute those phonorecords (3)—are not reserved exclusively to the copyright owner of a recorded musical work. When phonorecords of a musical work have been distributed to the public in the United States with the copyright owner's permission, any other person may obtain a license to make and distribute phonorecords of that musical work.[52] This is known as the *compulsory mechanical license* provision. That person, however, must notify the copyright owner and pay the royalty specified by the Copyright Act. For a discussion of the mechanical royalty rate, see chapter 4, "Income on Songs from Record Sales." Until January 1, 1983, the royalty rate was either 4 cents per song or ¾ cent per minute of playing time, whichever was larger. After that date, the rate increases as described in chapter 4.[53]

Royalties must be paid on every phonorecord made and distributed.[54]

The Copyright Act, however, provides that a person may obtain a compulsory mechanical license only "if his or her primary purpose in making phonorecords is to distribute them to the public for private use."[55] This qualification is important because it means that makers of background music systems (e.g., Muzak) must now obtain a license directly from the copyright owner, who is not forced to license the work and is not bound by the statutory royalty rate. This restriction also extends to manufacturers of phonorecords intended primarily for commercial use by broadcasters, discos, and juke box operators.[56]

Because the compulsory mechanical license procedures in the Copyright Act are costly and strict,[57] users generally attempt to negotiate voluntary licenses from the copyright owner of the musical work. Negotiated rates may be lower than the statutory royalty. To simplify the negotiating process of voluntary licensing, most copyright owners of musical works arrange for the Harry Fox Agency, Inc. (110 E. 59th Street, New York, N.Y. 10022; [212] 751-1930) to act as their agent in negotiating mechanical use royalties. So if you want to record a James Taylor song on your album, you contact the Harry Fox Agency. If the copyright owner of that song has authorized that organization to act as its licensing agent, then they may license you to record it. The royalty rates, although theoretically negotiable when dealing through the Harry Fox Agency, are standardized at the statutory rate; royalty payments for mechanical licenses are made quarterly to the Agency, which in turn distributes that royalty to the copyright owner, minus the Agency's fee.

The compulsory mechanical license includes the privilege of making an arrangement of the musical work to the extent necessary to conform it to the style or manner of interpretation of the performance. That arrangement, however, cannot change the basic melody or fundamental character of the musical work.[58] Also, that version of the musical work cannot be treated or protected as a derivative work without the copyright owner's express consent.[59]

LIMITATIONS ON EXCLUSIVE RIGHTS IN SOUND RECORDINGS

As with musical works, the Copyright Act also restricts the exclusive rights of the copyright owner of the sound recording. Of the five general rights listed earlier in this chapter, the right to publicly perform the sound recording (4) is not exclusive to the person having the copyright in the sound recording and may be enjoyed by anyone who obtains the phonorecords of the sound recording.[60]

Radio stations, for example, are considered to "publicly perform" both a song and the sound recording of a song every time they play a record over the air. Since the right to publicly perform is an exclusive right of the owner of a musical work (the song), the radio station must get permission and pay royalties.[61] But since the right to publicly perform is not an exclusive right of the owner of the copyright in the sound recording, no permission is required and no royalties are paid to the sound recording owner.[62] Remember: a song is a musical work separate from the work of the sound recording of the song. Congress is considering amending the Copyright Act to change this, but as the law currently stands, the owner of a sound recording is not entitled to royalties for the public performance of it.[63]

Obtaining a Copyright

CHAPTER
TWO

One question most frequently asked by songwriters is: "How can I keep my work from being stolen and how can I prove my ownership in the songs I have written?" There are various ways that proof of ownership can be obtained. The best form of proof is registration of your copyright claim with the Copyright Office in Washington, D.C.

Before discussing Copyright Office registration procedures and alternatives, it is important to understand the distinction between obtaining a copyright and registering or otherwise proving your claim of ownership. Obtaining your copyright is a very simple and easy process. You have to do nothing more than place the proper copyright notice on each copy of the song that is publicly distributed. The claim of copyright does not have to be registered with the Copyright Office (or anywhere else) to obtain a copyright. The Copyright Office does not "issue" or "grant" copyrights; it registers copyright claims. By putting the proper copyright notice on the copies of the work, the writer secures his or her copyright in the song and tells the rest of the world that he or she is the creator and copyright owner of the song.

NOTICE

The United States copyright notice has three elements: symbol, year, and owner.[1]

1. *Symbol.* For copies of all works except sound recordings, the first element is the word *Copyright,* the abbreviation *Copr.,* or the symbol ©.[2] Use of the symbol © also meets the notice requirements of certain foreign countries, so it is recommended.[3] Often you will see a notice utilizing both *Copyright* and ©. This is redundant and unnecessary, but does not invalidate the copyright notice.[4] For sound recordings (embodied in phonograph records and tapes, for example), the first element of the notice is the symbol ℗.[5] The rest of the elements are the same.
2. *Year.* The second element is the first year of publication of the work. Note that it is the year of first publication—not the year of creation—that must be included in the notice.[6] Later in this chapter we will discuss demo tapes and what year and notice you use for unpublished works.
3. *Owner.* The name of the owner of the copyright is the final element in the copyright notice. The name should be the present owner, not the original creator, if ownership has been transferred. Chapter 3 discusses the mechanics of transferring ownership in a copyright. By adding the words *All Rights Reserved,* additional international copyright protection is gained in Latin American countries under the Pan American Conventions, so their inclusion is advised.[7]

COPYRIGHT NOTICE FOR SONGS

The copyright notice for a copy of a musical work such as sheet music should take a form such as this:

© 1983 J. R. Mellowstone
All Rights Reserved.

A notice of this type should appear on the first page of each and every lead sheet for a song or piece of sheet music. In fact, whenever the song or even song lyrics appear on an album jacket, lyric sheet, record review, or elsewhere, a copyright notice should be utilized to protect the musical works. Although, technically, the copyright notice is required only when copies are published, we suggest it be used virtually every time the music or words are written out.

In chapter 1 we made the point that a phonorecord is not a *copy* of a musical work since you cannot visually perceive the song from the phonorecord. This is important because the copyright notice is required only on published copies, and consequently it is not necessary to place a copyright notice for the songs on a phonorecord in order to protect the songs.[8] While the owner of the songs on a record is generally identified on the record jacket, this is primarily so royalties on mechanical use and performances are properly paid. Chapter 4 explains these royalties more fully.

COPYRIGHT NOTICE FOR SOUND RECORDINGS

Record albums, tapes, and other phonorecords require a notice of the following type in order to protect the sound recording:

℗ 1983 BOOGIE RECORDS
All Rights Reserved.

It is common practice in the music industry for this notice to appear on both the bottom rear of the jacket and on the label of record albums. The law, however, requires only that the notice be affixed to the phonorecord or its label or container.[9]

COPYRIGHT NOTICE FOR RECORD ALBUM LINER NOTES AND ARTWORK

A record album jacket often contains elaborate artwork and liner notes and itself is a work distinct from the songs and sound recording. As such, it can be separately copyrighted. The Copyright Office, however, advises that when the owner of the sound recording also owns the rights in the album cover, and the sound recording and cover are registered together, the only notice that is required is the ℗ notice on the cover.[10] The single notice covers both the sound recording and the accompanying printed materials. Most major record companies take the more conservative approach and include both a ℗ and © on album covers. This indicates that the company is claiming rights in both the sound recording and the cover art and text.

Whenever the owner of some aspect of the cover is different from the owner of the sound recording, a separate © notice for that aspect is required. An example of this situation is where a photographer agrees to have a picture included on the jacket, but he wants to retain copyright ownership of the photograph so he can use it for other purposes. In this case, a notice with the ©, year, and name of photographer should appear on or just beside the photograph. The photographer will want to separately register the photograph.

OPTIONAL INFORMATION

The only notice that the Copyright Act requires is the three-part notice consisting of symbol, year, and owner. Record albums and sheet music, however, often contain additional information. As mentioned above, the words *All rights reserved* generally appear. Also, record albums and sheet music usually list the names of the original songwriters. Records also identify which performing rights society (BMI, ASCAP, or SESAC) licenses the song for broadcast and live performance. Chapter 4 discusses these organizations and how they operate.

Whenever a work contains copyrighted works belonging to other owners, the words *Used by permission* are usually included in addition to the copyright notice of the other owner. You also occasionally see language on a record album such as: "Unauthorized reproduction is prohibited. Violators will be subject to civil and criminal penalties." As you will see when you read chapter 5 on infringement, this threat is inherent in the protection that copyright law provides, so the language does not add any substantive rights. Still, it is not harmful and may deter an occasional infringer. The listing of playing times for singles or album cuts is primarily for the convenience of disc jockeys. The address of the record company is also required under the law of at least one state, New York.

SUMMARY OF COPYRIGHT NOTICES APPEARING ON RECORD ALBUMS

As you can see, there are a variety of copyright notices and other information that must appear on a record album. Just to recap, a list follows of what you will find on most albums.

Item	*Location*	*Purpose*
℗, year, owner	Typically on label and rear of jacket	Gives notice of owner of sound recording; also gives notice of owner of album art and text unless another owner is identified
©, year, owner	Label, rear of jacket	Provides extra notice of ownership of the art and text on the cover and label when the owner of the sound recording is the same
©, year, owner	Beside specific text or art on jacket	Identifies ownership of specific text or art when they are owned by another
©, year, owner	At end of written lyrics when they appear on jacket or lyric sheet	Provides notice of ownership of songs
All rights reserved	After each © notice	Provides notice required for copyright protection in certain foreign countries
Used by permission	After certain © notices	Used whenever permission to use another's copyrighted work is granted

Some of these items are optional, and there is some variation in how they are handled. Examine several commercial albums, and you will see many of the variations. By the way, you will not find a ℗ on phonorecords manufactured before 1972. The law authorizing the notice did not go into effect until February 15, 1972.[11]

Although there is variation in the information appearing on albums, for anyone manufacturing albums we recommend including the item if there is any doubt as to

Item	*Location*	*Purpose*
Unauthorized reproduction prohibited, etc.	Rear of jacket	An optional warning designed to deter infringement; can take various forms
Songwriter names	Adjacent to song titles on index of songs	Not required by copyright law when songwriters have assigned songs to music publishers or others, but it is customarily added as a matter of courtesy or may be required by contract, and it facilitates payment of songwriter royalties
BMI or ASCAP or SESAC	Next to song title	Not part of the copyright notice but serves to identify the performing rights society that licenses the song for public performances and that collects royalties
Playing time	Next to song title	Convenience to disc jockeys who have to squeeze in those ten-second commercial spots
Address of record company	Rear of jacket	Required in some states

whether it is necessary. Omitting a copyright notice is much more dangerous than having redundant notices.

DEMO TAPES

Frequently, a songwriter or musician will prepare demonstration tapes of material to submit to record companies, agents, or others in the music industry. Lead sheets and demo 45's are also often used this way. The purpose of these demos is to provide a sample of the material, and using a demo in this manner generally is not a *publication* of the work under the Copyright Act.[12]

Because the musical work and sound recording are not being published, technically you are not required to put a copyright notice on demos. If a song is on a cassette or demo 45, the musical work is not visually perceivable and, for that reason also, no notice is required. Nonetheless we think it is a good idea to use a ℗ notice on every demo recording and a © notice on every copy of sheet music. It identifies you as claiming rights in the works and avoids problems if somehow the demo or sheet music is published. As we discussed above, the Copyright Act requires that the notice contain the year of publication.[13] Since there is no year of publication for a demo, use the year the demos are first sent out. When using cassettes, put the notice right on the cassette, not just on the box. Sheet music should have the copyright notice on the first page of every song.

EFFECTS OF OMITTING COPYRIGHT NOTICE

Under former copyright law, omission of a copyright notice would automatically forfeit protection and throw the work into the public domain. This is not true under the new Act, which provides that a work published without copyright notice has at least some statutory protection for five years.[14] The new Act offers certain curative provisions when a copyright notice is defective or omitted. Briefly, these provide that when the name or date or the entire notice is omitted, copyright protection still can be obtained if:

1. the notice has been omitted from no more than a "relatively small number" of copies distributed to the public; or
2. the work is registered no later than five years after the publication without notice took place, and a reasonable effort is made "to add the notice to all copies distributed" in the United States after the omission has been discovered; or
3. the notice has been omitted by another in violation of an express agreement to place the notice on all publicly distributed copies.[15]

Although omission of the notice does not result in invalidating the copyright, innocent infringers who were misled by the lack of notice may not be liable for damages.[16] Also, there is no clear meaning for the quoted language in items (1) and (2) above since there has been very little litigation interpreting that language. Until the language has been interpreted, you can never be certain that your omission of the copyright notice falls within the scope of that language. In other words, a defective notice does not necessarily result in loss of the copyright, but because it is the fundamental step in securing a copyright, every effort should be made to do it correctly.

REGISTRATION

Reasons to Register With the Copyright Office. There are certain important benefits made available to a copyright owner by registering the copyright claim with the Copyright Office. The primary benefit is actually more in the nature of a requirement. An owner is not permitted to file an infringement action until the copyrighted work has been registered with the Copyright Office, even if the work is being infringed. Once the copyright claim has been registered with the Copyright Office, then the Act authorizes the owner to file suit.

The Act gives the owner what is known as a *prima facie* presumption of ownership. Essentially, the statute authorizes a court to presume that the registered copyright claimant is the actual owner of the copyrighted work. The burden of proof is shifted to the infringer to disprove the ownership of the copyright claimant.

The Copyright Act grants additional incentives to register a copyright claim before infringement. First, the statute authorizes a court to award statutory damages rather than actual damages to a successful copyright claimant. In an infringement action when a plaintiff sues a defendant for money damages, the plaintiff must prove exactly what his or her damages were in dollars and cents. That sum would be actual damages. Proof of actual damages can be time-consuming and therefore costly since litigation costs are high. If, however, the plaintiff has to document only the infringement and ownership, the court is then authorized to find a damage award for the plaintiff in an amount no less than $250 per infringement and no more than $10,000 per infringement. If willfulness is proven, the ceiling on the award increases to $50,000 per infringement. The dollars to be awarded, therefore, can add up very fast, and the costly need to prove actual damages is eliminated. With an award of statutory damages, the burden is on the defendant to persuade a court that any damages suffered by the plaintiff were too small to justify any award above the minimum. By placing this burden on the defendant, his or her costs of defense also are increased. Of course, to award damages the court must first find copyright ownership and an infringement.

Another advantage of registering before any infringement is that the plaintiff, on a successful verdict, is allowed to recover reasonable attorneys' fees and costs, with the unsuccessful defendant being required to pay for fees and costs. It is easy to see that there are some very real benefits to be gained from registering a copyright claim with the Copyright Office.

As an aside, should the infringement occur within three months after the publication of the copyrighted work but before registration, then so long as the registration is made before the end of that three-month period after publication the additional benefits described here will still be available.

You can register a work, whether it is published or unpublished, by filing the following with the Copyright Office:

1. an application on a form supplied by the Copyright Office
2. a $10 fee
3. two copies of the work (one copy, if the work is unpublished).[17]

APPLICATION FORMS

Copyright application forms can be obtained free of charge by writing to the U.S. Copyright Office, Library of Congress, Washington, D.C. 20559. You also can place an order for application forms by calling the Copyright Office at (202) 287-9100. Information specialists, who can take orders, are on duty from 8:00 A.M. to 7:00 P.M. Eastern time, Monday through Friday. A telephone recorder has also been installed so forms and circulars may be ordered after hours. The recorder is in operation after 7:00 P.M. weekdays and throughout the weekend.

You must use an original Copyright Office form to register a copyright. Photocopies are unacceptable.

REGISTERING SONGS

The application form for songs is Form PA. It is used for all published and unpublished works of performing arts (hence "PA"), including musical and dramatic works, pantomimes and choreographic works, motion pictures, and other audiovisual works. Form PA has replaced old Form E for songs. In the Appendix of this book, you will find a copy of Form PA together with instructions for completing it.

When using Form PA to register copyrights in songs, you should submit two lead sheets for deposit if the song has already been published as lead sheets or in some other visually perceivable form. If the published musical work exists only as a phonorecord, two copies of the best edition of the phonorecord should accompany the application for registration.[18] This rule means that if your song has never been transcribed, you can send in two cassette tapes or other phonorecords and satisfy the Copyright Office's requirements. Accepting cassettes is a major change from the pre-January 1, 1978, provision that required transcribed music.

Remember, if neither copies nor phonorecords of a musical work exist, then the work has not been fixed and cannot be copyrighted until it is reduced to a tangible form—either transcribed copies or phonorecords. A performer who plays his own songs live from memory cannot register them until they are recorded or written down.[19]

Registering More Than One Song. The regulations of the Copyright Office permit the owner of songs to register a number of those songs in one filing for a single $10 fee, whether by lead sheet, record, or tape. If you select this process for your songs, the following procedure is recommended:

1. If you use tape, identify yourself on the tape by name; indicate the number of songs that are on the tape; recite the number and title for each song before recording it on the tape; perform the song; when finished, state that the song is completed; recite the number and title of the next song, repeating the same procedure until you have recorded all the songs you wish to register (or you have run out of tape).
2. You will have to identify the compilation of songs by a single title on the PA form. For example, "Collective Compositions of Stan Hitmaker, Series I." Each of the PA registration forms has a continuation sheet ("PA/CON") with blank spaces. It is recommended that the titles of the individual songs be listed in the bottom blank space in the same sequence they are recorded on the tape.

If you want to file a claim of ownership in a sound recording along with your songs, you could use an SR form instead of the PA form for your songs and the sound recording, identifying yourself as the author of the sound recording, words, and music.

This procedure will work only if you are the owner of all the songs on the tape (and the sound recording if you also are registering your copyright claim in that). You cannot group different owners of different songs on the same tape. If there is more than one owner of the songs (and, if relevant, the sound recording) and they are the same owners for all the songs (and sound recording, if relevant), you can still use this procedure. Because the group of songs is registered as a collection, only the collection title will appear in the catalogs and indexes of the Copyright Office. Some attorneys and music publishers are not in favor of this process because it may complicate segregating one of the songs from the group of songs on a subsequent copyright transfer of just one of the songs, such as with a publishing agreement. On the surface, this may be a problem. Careful drafting, however, specifically identifying the song to be transferred, can eliminate that concern.

One other drawback with this procedure is that the titles of the individual songs will not be indexed and cross-referenced to your name as author. Consequently, somebody trying to identify you as an author of one of the songs listed as a group would not be able to locate you because the song itself is not separately indexed. One way of overcoming this situation is to do a follow-up registration on what is known as a CA form. On this form you could request the Copyright Office to separately index the titles of each of the songs listed in the earlier registration and have that separate indexing cross-referenced to your name and the number assigned to that earlier registration. You must wait, however, until you receive the initial PA form registration from the Copyright Office so you can refer on the CA form to the registration number issued by the Copyright Office on the PA form. The fee for this procedure is $10 for the CA form plus 50 cents for each title separately indexed. Even with the additional filing fee and per title charge, the aggregate cost will be far less than registering each song separately.

REGISTERING SOUND RECORDINGS

The form used for registering a copyright in a sound recording is Form SR. A copy of this form and its instructions is found in the Appendix. When using Form SR, two copies of the best edition of the sound recording should accompany the registration. The jacket and all other printed material published with the sound recording should be sent with the phonorecord and, when the owner of it is the same as the owner of the sound recording, it is registered simultaneously.

Occasionally a single copyright owner will have the rights both in the musical works and the sound recordings embodied in a phonorecord. An example is a performer who records and releases an independent album of original songs. In these circumstances, Form SR may be used to register copyrights in both works simultaneously (see discussion above regarding registration of a group of songs on Form PA).[20] Two copies of the best edition of the sound recording should accompany the registration. A single $10 fee covers the entire application, regardless of the number of songs on the recording.

REGISTRATION OF ALBUM JACKETS

When for some reason the owner of some or all of the printed material accompanying a phonorecord is different from the owner of the sound recording, the printed materials can be separately registered. The application forms are Form TX (which covers non-dramatic literary works or texts) or Form VA (which covers works of visual arts). The choice of which form you should use depends on whether the material is mainly textual or mainly pictorial, although the form under which the work is copyrighted will not affect the validity of the copyright.[21] Copies of those forms can be obtained from the Copyright Office in Washington, D.C.

THE FEE

The $10 fee for initial registration of a copyright is the same regardless of the type of work or form used. It should be in the form of a check or money order payable to the Register of Copyrights.[22] The Copyright Office accepts personal checks.

UNPUBLISHED WORKS

When registering unpublished works, one copy or phonorecord of the work must accompany the registration form. If the unpublished work exists only as a phonorecord, deposit of one phonorecord is required with the application for registration. If the unpublished work exists in both copies and phonorecords, the form best representing the work should be deposited with the application. This usually is the written copy.[23]

FILING THE REGISTRATION

The completed application form, the fee, and the copies should be packaged together and sent to: U.S. Copyright Office, Library of Congress, Washington, D.C. 20559. Ordinarily it is not necessary to send the package by registered mail; first class mail is sufficient. Remember to keep a copy of the work you deposit.

Do not become overanxious if the Copyright Office does not immediately return a certificate of copyright to you. It processes over six hundred thousand applications a year and a delay of three or four months in sending out certificates is not unusual. Also, the effective date of the registration is the date the Copyright Office received all the required material, regardless of how long thereafter it takes to process the application and mail the certificate. Assuming you followed the steps outlined here, you eventually will get a certificate with a registration number. You will want to hold on to that piece of paper for a long time, so give some careful thought to where you want to keep it.

Getting a certificate is a significant step in copyright protection, but it is not absolute protection. Remember that the Copyright Office makes no effort to see if your song is similar or even identical to a song already registered. It simply determines if the work is of the type suitable for copyright protection and whether the formalities of the notice were followed. If the song is an infringement, registering it does not cleanse the infringement.

ALTERNATIVES TO REGISTRATION

As we explained earlier, placing the copyright notice on a work secures the copyright, and registration is not required. As noted, though, registration does have benefits —not the least of which is that it makes proof of copyright ownership much easier. If you are forced to sue, this saves some legal fees. Nonetheless, the $10 registration fee is a major financial obstacle to many songwriters, particularly those who have composed a large number of songs and do not want to use the group registration discussed above.

We are hesitant to recommend anything short of maximum protection, but if cost is an important concern, you should know that there are a variety of alternative routes you can take, each with certain risks.

One choice is to postpone registering until the song is about to be recorded or otherwise published. The primary disadvantage of this course of action is that if the song is ripped off and registered by another person before you register, you will have a more difficult time proving that you are the rightful owner and that the other person is the infringer. Nevertheless, many songwriters do not register their songs before sending them to publishers. If the publisher picks up the song, then it takes care of registration. If you go this route, do put a copyright ℗ notice and your name on the demos before sending them to anyone.

The use of a "poor man's" copyright entails mailing yourself a copy of a tape or lead sheets of your song by certified mail. On receipt of that certified mailing, the addressee (you) does not open it. Instead, the package is put away. If an infringement action is ever filed and the case goes to trial, the plaintiff (you) could introduce the sealed package as evidence of ownership. This approach has some merit in that it does document a claim of ownership at a point in time. The court must first be convinced, however, that you properly mailed the package to yourself and that it had never been tampered with or opened while in your possession. In effect, you must rely solely on your own testimony. Also, none of the benefits of Copyright Office registration discussed earlier would be available to you under a "poor man's" copyright.

For some years Songwriter's Resources and Services (SRS) has provided a service allowing composers to register with the SRS taped copies of their compositions. For a charge of $5 for the first song and $1 for each additional song (SRS members get a 25 percent discount), SRS, on receipt of your tape, will file it in a secure location and record the date of its receipt, which is certified and maintained in its files under your name. You should submit your tape with the songs identified in a cover letter or an SRS form and identify yourself by name and address. SRS returns a certificate of registration to you for your files and information.

In the event a claim of copyright infringement arises, a representative of SRS would be made available to testify to its receipt of your tape and the identified song on that tape. This SRS testimony would be bona fide third-party proof of ownership at a point in time. This approach has the advantage of your not being required to rely solely on your own testimony for proof of ownership and is very useful. SRS registration will not, however, satisfy the requirement that your copyright claim be registered with the Copyright Office before you can bring an infringement suit; nor will it provide for the award of statutory damages and attorneys' fees if the infringement occurs before you register your claim with the Copyright Office.

Another form of registration is provided by American Song Festival's American Protection Service (APS); its service is patterned after that of SRS.

SRS's address is 6301 Hollywood Blvd., Hollywood, Calif. 90028. APS's address is P.O. Box 57, Hollywood, Calif. 90028.

DEPOSIT

Even if you decide not to register your copyright claim, the Copyright Act still imposes a requirement on the copyright owner to deposit two copies of all published works with the Library of Congress. This deposit requirement, however, is not a precondition to copyright protection.[24] Your copyright is secure so long as you used the notice properly. Failure to deposit does not jeopardize those rights.

Within three months of placing a work bearing the copyright notice on sale or distributing it by renting, leasing, lending, or some other form of distribution, the owner of the copyright must make a deposit with the Copyright Office. The deposit is for use by the Library of Congress and requires submission of two complete copies of the visually perceptible work or two copies of phonorecords of the sound recording, together with any printed or visually perceptible material printed with the phonorecord.

If the musical work is published both in the form of copies and phonorecords, two transcribed copies (not phonorecords) of the best edition should be deposited. Lead sheets generally are used to satisfy this deposit requirement.

The mandatory deposit provisions apply only when the work is published—that is, placed on sale or distributed by renting, leasing, lending, or some other method. When the musical work is unpublished, deposit is not required by law.

If the deposit is not made, the Register of Copyrights may make written demand for the deposit. Failure to make the deposit within three months after the demand makes the copyright owner liable for fines of $250 and the retail price of the copies.[25] In cases of willful or repeated failure, an additional fine of $2,500 can be imposed.[26] Remember, however, that neglecting or failing to make the mandatory deposit has no effect on the validity of the copyright.

If you do register your work by filing the proper application form (PA or SR), then the copies or phonorecords that you submit with your registration application also satisfy the deposit requirement, and you do not have to deposit a second set of copies or phonorecords.[27]

Duration and Transfer of the Copyright

CHAPTER
THREE

DURATION

One of the major changes made by the Copyright Act is the duration of the copyright. Under the former federal law, copyright protection began at the date of publication, lasted for twenty-eight years, then could be renewed for another twenty-eight-year period.[1] This duration period still applies to all copyrighted works published before January 1, 1978. Under the new Copyright Act, copyright protection begins upon creation (that is, when the work is first fixed) and extends, in most cases, for the life of the author plus an additional fifty years after the author's death.[2] If you create a song in 1980 and die in the year 2001, the copyright will terminate in 2051. The duration period under the new Act applies (a) to works created on or after January 1, 1978, and (b) to works created on or before January 1, 1978, but registered as unpublished or not published as of that date.[3]

For joint works created on or after January 1, 1978, when the work was not for hire, the term of the copyright consists of the life of the last surviving author plus fifty years after that author's death.[4]

A work that is created by an anonymous author, or for which the author has used an assumed name (a *pseudonymous work*), or that has been done for hire has a copyright duration of seventy-five years from the year of first publication or one hundred years from the year of creation, whichever expires first.[5] If a song is created in 1985 and is first published in 1990, the term of the copyright will expire in 2065, which is seventy-five years from the date of first publication. Had the same song first been published in 2015, the term of the copyright would expire in 2085, which is one hundred years from the date of creation, rather than 2090, which is seventy-five years from the date of first publication.

COPYRIGHT DURATION
FOR WORKS FOR HIRE

Created (C)	*Published (P)*	*P + 75*	*C + 100*	*Expires*
1985	1990	2065	2085	2065
1985	2015	2090	2085	2085

If the identity of the author of an anonymous or pseudonymous work is revealed before the expiration of its copyright term, then the duration will be the life of that author plus fifty years.[6]

Copyrights registered under the former federal law that were in their first twenty-eight-year term on January 1, 1978, will continue for that original twenty-eight-year period. Even under the new Act, renewal still will be required for these works during the twenty-eighth year of the original term of the copyright. The renewal term for such works, however, will be forty-seven years instead of twenty-eight years,[7] for a total duration of seventy-five years.

For a copyrighted work that was already in its renewal term before January 1, 1978, the duration of the copyright automatically is extended to last for seventy-five years from the year the copyright first became effective.[8] So if the work were first copyrighted and registered in 1945 and the copyright registration renewed in 1973, the copyright would finally expire in the year 2020 (1973–1945 = 28; 1945 + 75 = 2020).

After copyright protection expires, the work goes into the public domain and anyone may freely use it without any obligation to the former copyright owner. There is no need to obtain the permission of Francis Scott Key's heirs before using Key's original music. You can claim a copyright in an original arrangement of a public domain work. Therefore, you would have to obtain permission of the arranger before using a contemporary copyrighted arrangement of Key, assuming the arrangement has been copyrighted and its copyright has not expired. (See chapter 5, "Avoiding Infringement.")

TRANSFER OF OWNERSHIP

The ownership of a copyright or any of its divisible parts may be transferred by any type of property transfer, including contract, lease, license, or gift.[9] The exclusive rights described in chapter 1 that are parts of a copyright may be transferred and owned separately. For example, while retaining other rights, a songwriter could give Muzak a license to publicly broadcast his or her song in the United States for a fee.

We should point out that copyright ownership is distinct from the ownership of any material object embodying a work,[10] and transfer of the ownership of such a material object does not convey a copyright. For example, if you buy the album *Saturday Night Fever,* you have not obtained any rights in the copyright for the sound recording or the musical works. You have purchased only the ownership right in the phonorecord; you can resell the album or give it away, but you cannot reproduce it. At the same time, the transfer of copyright ownership does not convey a property right in any material object embodying the copyrighted work. You can sell a copyright without selling any of the phonorecords embodying the copyrighted work.

A songwriter who signs a publishing agreement with a publisher for one of his or her songs transfers the ownership and therefore the copyright in that song to the publisher. If the publisher fails to publish the song (for example, fails to get it recorded by an artist or used in a film), and the publisher's agreement does not include a reversion clause permitting the writer to take back the copyright in the event of non-publication, the writer will not be able to retrieve the copyright in the song unless the publisher voluntarily returns it.

EXECUTION AND RECORDING OF TRANSFERS

To be effective, a transfer of copyright ownership must be in writing, and signed by the owner or the owner's agent.[11] The transfer document must contain the signature of the person who executed the transfer or be accompanied by a sworn certificate that it is a true copy of the original.[12]

Filing the transfer document with the Copyright Office is important, since recording the transfer is a prerequisite to instituting an infringement action.[13] After recording the transfer, the new copyright owner may sue for any infringement that occurred prior to the recording of the transfer with the Copyright Office.[14] This being so, when a copyright or one of its component parts is transferred to you, the transfer agreement should state specifically that the right to sue for previous infringement of the copyright is transferred with the copyright itself.

Immediately recording the transfer with the Copyright Office is especially important since conflicts may emerge between different persons claiming the same right in a copyright by way of a transfer from the prior copyright owner. The first one to record with the Copyright Office prevails.[15]

The following examples illustrate how the transfer concept works:

1. John Gifted has registered his copyright in one of his songs, "Dance Until It Hurts." CBS Songs signs John to a songwriter-publisher agreement. CBS Songs gets Billy Joel to record the song. The agreement that John signs conveys all rights in the song to CBS Songs and grants John a 50 percent songwriter's royalty in the revenue that CBS Songs generates from its promotion of the song. For CBS Songs to secure its rights to sue for any infringement of the song, it would have to record the transfer with the Copyright Office.
2. "Dance Until It Hurts" becomes a smash and John is inspired to write a sequel song, "The Hurt Dance Glide." John offers to assign the song to CBS Songs before he registers his copyright in the song. CBS Songs accepts the song and enters into another agreement with John. CBS Songs then registers a copyright claim (Form PA), citing John as the author and itself as the claimant, explaining it acquired the rights to the song by way of the agreement with John. At the same time that CBS Songs files the copyright registration (Form PA), it also should file a transfer document. A separate $10 fee must be paid for each filing.

TERMINATION OF TRANSFERS

The provisions for termination of licenses and other transfers of interests in a copyright are substantially changed by the Copyright Act.[16] These termination provisions are very complex, and there are many variations that could occur which cannot be fully developed in this book. You should consult with an attorney before implementing any plans to execute your termination rights.

Under the former federal law, a copyright existed for two separate terms of twenty-eight years each, assuming a renewal was filed for the second twenty-eight-year term.[17] If the copyright owner transferred his or her rights during the copyright's first twenty-eight-year term, such rights could not be taken back by the owner during that term ("the twenty-eight-year rule").[18]

On the expiration of the first term under the twenty-eight-year rule, the transferring copyright owner could terminate the transfer and negotiate a new agreement for the second term of the copyright, even though the initial transfer included the second twenty-eight-year term.[19] In other words, at the end of the first twenty-eight years the copyright automatically returned to the transferring owner. This return was designed to protect an author who would be unable to predict whether the copyright would be valuable in the future. The twenty-eight-year rule still applies to all copyrights that became effective before January 1, 1978.[20]

Since the Act extends the copyright duration period of pre-January 1, 1978, works to seventy-five years from that work's effective copyright date, the transfer of any copyrighted work in its renewed or extended twenty-eight-year term may be terminated at any time during the five-year period beginning at the end of fifty-six years from the date the copyright was originally secured, or beginning on January 1, 1978, whichever date is later ("the fifty-six-year rule").[21] If the work were copyrighted in 1922 and renewed in 1950, then the transfer may be terminated during the five-year period of 1978 to 1983. The termination notice must be served no later than two years and no sooner than ten years before the termination date and must be recorded in the Copyright Office.[22]

Under the new Act, since copyrights last for the author's life plus fifty years and there is no renewal period, there is no automatic return of the transferred copyright to the original owner. Consequently, the new Act allows the transferor to elect to terminate any transfer within a limited period of time ("the thirty-five-year rule").[23]

The thirty-five-year rule establishes two separate time periods for termination of the transfer. When the transfer does not include the right of publication, that transfer (the thirty-five-year rule) may be terminated at any time during the five-year period that begins at the end of thirty-five years from the date of the execution of the transfer.

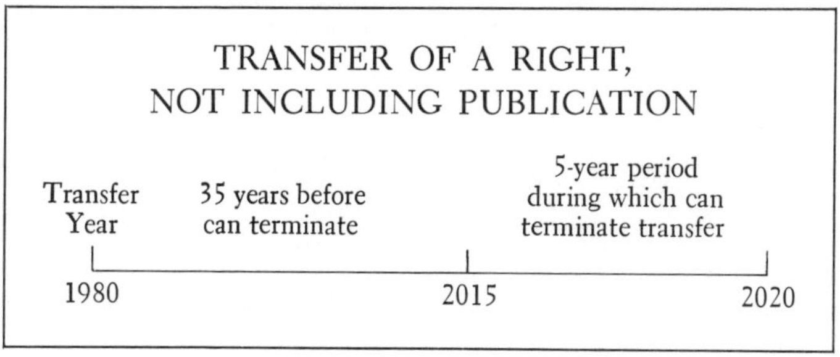

If the transfer includes the right to publish the work, the five-year period within which the transfer may be terminated begins (a) at the end of thirty-five years from the date of the first publication of the work under the transfer, or (b) at the end of forty years from the date of execution of the transfer, whichever term of years ends first.[24] For example, if in 1980 you transfer publishing rights in your song to CBS Songs and the song is published in 1981, then you may terminate that transfer between the years 2016 and 2021, or between the thirty-fifth and fortieth years of the publication date in 1981. If the song transferred in 1980 is not published until 1990, then you may terminate the grant between the years 2020 and 2025, or between the fortieth and forty-fifth years of the date of the transfer in 1980. In other words, if as a songwriter you sell a song to a publisher, you or your heirs will have the right to get it back—eventually.

TRANSFER OF A RIGHT,
INCLUDING PUBLICATION

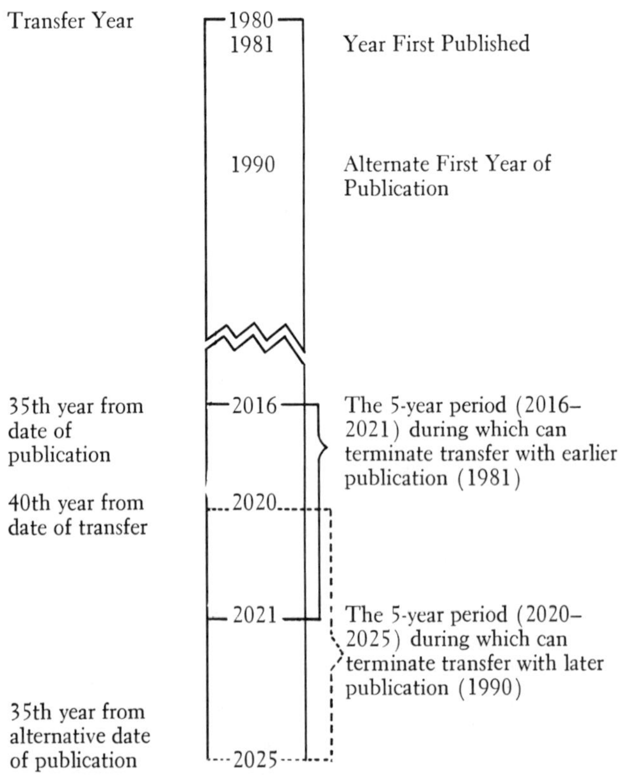

The transferor or his or her successor terminates a transfer by signing and giving the transferee or its successor an advance written notice of termination.[25] The notice:

1. must state the effective date of the termination, which must be during the five-year period mentioned in the preceding paragraph
2. must be served on the transferee or successor not less than two years nor more than ten years before the termination is to become effective
3. must be recorded in the Copyright Office before the effective date of termination.[26]

For example, if a song (including the right to publish) was transferred in 1980 and first published in 1981, then:

1. termination may be effective at any time between the years 2016 and 2021
2. assuming the grant is to terminate at the end of the thirty-five-year period (2016) from date of publication (1981), the notice of termination must be sent between the years 2006 and 2014
3. the notice of termination must be filed with the Copyright Office before the termination date.

On the effective date of termination, all rights covered by the terminated license or transfer revert to the author or his or her successors.[27] If the grant is not terminated, then the original transfer continues in effect for the term of the transferred work's copyright provided for under the Act.[28] The transferring owner cannot convey or agree to convey any right covered by an existing grant until the termination of that grant has been completed.[29]

Remember: the termination must be filed so there

is a public record that the transferor and not the transferee once again owns the rights to the song.

An important point to remember is that when all of the copyright interests in a song have been transferred, each of the component or divisible parts of the copyright in that song also have been transferred, including the right to make derivative works. These divisible parts of a copyrighted work were discussed earlier in chapter 1, "Rights Provided by Copyright."

The termination of a transfer will not of itself, however, terminate the right of the transferee to continue to use and enjoy the benefits of any derivative work that was based on the original copyrighted work.[30] Terminating the transferee's right to continue to exploit the derivative work can be accomplished only by the transferor's specifically retaining the right in the transfer agreement to terminate the transferee's enjoyment of the derivative work upon the termination of the initial transfer. For example, if a publishing company, to which the copyright in John Gifted's song "The Hurt Dance Glide" has been transferred, uses an instrumental arrangement of that song in the sound track of a movie that it is producing, such a use would constitute a derivative work. If John Gifted or his heirs terminated the transfer within the time period permitted under the Act, John or his heirs could bar the publishing company from using the song after the termination date—but they could not stop the company from continuing to use the song on the sound track unless the transfer agreement specifically and in writing authorized the transferor to terminate any derivative uses of the song. Obtaining such a provision would be unusual, but the language that would cover this situation might read as follows: "Songwriter retains the right to terminate this transfer of the song 'The Hurt Dance Glide,' including the right to use the song in any derivative work, in accordance with the provisions of the 1976 Copyright Act."

Income from Music

CHAPTER
FOUR

The preceding chapters explored the legal elements of copyright—what it is and how to obtain it. We now turn to the ways the copyright owner can benefit financially from the work. The primary sources of this benefit are phonograph record sales, sales of sheet music, use of music in film and video, performances before a live audience, and performances through the broadcast media. Since the sales of sheet music of popular songs are relatively small today, in this chapter we will concentrate the discussion on income from recording and performing. Because of the importance of music in films, we also mention financial arrangements for movie sound tracks.

RIGHTS IN A SONG

Before a song is recorded on an album in today's popular music industry, the songwriter (or the lyricist and composer together, in the case of a joint work) generally assigns the copyright in the song to a music publisher. The assignment agreement—or songwriter contract, as it is often called—provides that the publisher will become the owner of the copyright and the songwriter will receive a percentage of the income from the song. The terms of the songwriter contract are negotiable, but most agreements provide for a 50–50 split of income between publisher and songwriter. Occasionally a songwriter receives a cash advance from the publisher, which is recouped out of future royalties on the song. Often the publisher deducts an administration fee of between 10 and 20 percent of the gross receipts before splitting the remaining income. Some agreements also provide that unless the publisher actually publishes the song through release in a phonograph record or use in a film sound track or generates a specified minimum in royalty income within a given period of time (e.g., one year), the ownership of the copyright reverts to the songwriter.

In earlier days of the music industry, the publisher earned its share of the income by promoting the song and attempting to persuade a major act to record it (finding a "cover"). The structure of the industry has changed, however, and often today music publishers perform no promotional services. Either songs go directly from songwriter to performer, or the performer writes his or her own songs. While it is still common for an independent publisher to be involved, songwriters and recording companies frequently avoid independent publishers. A device typically used is for the songwriter (who also may be the performer) to create his or her own publishing company. Record companies also own publishing companies; CBS, for example, owns CBS Songs.

In the case of a songwriter-performer entering into a record deal with a major label, the song often will be published by the songwriter's own publishing company, or by the record company's publisher, or co-published by both (with the publisher's share of the income being divided between the publishing companies of the performer and the record company). The outcome is that an artist who writes lyrics and music and also has a publishing company will have royalty rights for each of those roles. The artist, for example, might collect 50 percent of the copyright income in the songwriter role and an additional 25 percent in a co-publisher role.

INCOME ON SONGS FROM RECORD SALES

When a phonograph record (or prerecorded tape) is sold at retail, the song copyright owner is entitled to receive a license fee for the mechanical use of each song on the phonorecord. Essentially the term *mechanical use* refers to every phonorecord made and distributed. This mechanical use fee is guaranteed under the compulsory licensing provisions of the Copyright Act[1] discussed in chapter 1. The Act provided for a set license fee of 4 cents (or ¾ cent per minute of playing time, or fraction thereof, whichever is greater) for each song on a phonorecord that was distributed between July 1981 and December 1982. The rate increased to 4¼ cents (or .8 cent per minute of playing time) on January 1, 1983, and to 4½ cents (or .85 cent per minute of playing time) on July 1, 1984. The rate increases again on January 1, 1986, to 5 cents (or .95 cent per minute of playing time).[2] The copyright owner and licensee, however, can voluntarily agree to increase or decrease this fee. Many songs are voluntarily licensed through the Harry Fox Agency, an organization established by music publishers that acts as the interface between the record manufacturers and many publishers in the United States (see page 15). For a charge of between 3 and 4½ percent of the fees collected, the Harry Fox Agency makes arrangements with record companies to grant mechanical licenses and collects license fees for records manufactured and distributed, and remits them to publishers. This arrangement relieves publishers and record companies from tracking each other down, serves to centralize the bookkeeping, and avoids the procedural complications of compulsory mechanical licensing. Mechanical license collection can also be handled by individual songwriters or publishers.

In the typical situation, assuming a license fee of 4

cents per song, the songwriter will receive about 2 cents for each album sold with one of his songs on it. The publisher (which also may be the songwriter and/or the record company) will get the other approximately 2 cents. If the songwriter wrote ten songs on one album, his income would rise to 20 cents per album sold (plus in some cases an equal amount for the songwriter's role as a publisher).

The basic mechanical royalty rate was 2 cents until January 1, 1978. It was increased to 2¾ cents, before being raised again in July 1981. Because of the large increase in the statutory mechanical rate, many record companies attempt to negotiate a lower rate with publishers. The Act does not prohibit this, and record companies often try to obtain mechanical licenses for 3 cents or some other reduced rate.

INCOME ON SONGS FROM PUBLIC PERFORMANCE

Under the Copyright Act, a radio or television broadcast, like a live concert, is a public performance, and no one can publicly perform a copyrighted song for profit without the permission of the song copyright owner.[3]

As a practical matter, songwriters and their publishers grant this permission to perform their songs through one of the performing rights organizations—usually Broadcast Music Incorporated (BMI), the American Society of Composers, Authors and Publishers (ASCAP), or the Society of European Songwriters, Authors and Composers (SESAC). ASCAP, founded in 1914, is the oldest of these organizations. BMI was not established until 1941, but today is the largest of the organizations.

A publisher and songwriter each enter agreements with one of these performing rights organizations to permit the organization to license nondramatic public performances of the composition. Because the license fees are small and the number of songs broadcast almost imponderable, neither individual songs nor performances are licensed. Rather, BMI, ASCAP, and SESAC generally enter broad arrangements with radio stations, television stations, theaters, clubs, and schools, permitting them to use any material in the performing rights organization's catalogs as often as they like in exchange for a blanket license fee. The fee for radio and TV stations is usually based on the user's gross income. Restaurants, clubs, and schools pay on the basis of several factors—including capacity, cover charge, and annual entertainment budget.

The performing rights organizations theoretically divide the license fees they receive among their publishers and writers on the basis of how often the songs are performed. The difficulty in monitoring every radio and TV broadcast and public concert, however, forces the performing rights societies to use sampling techniques to determine approximate airplay and to split performance receipts on that basis. The sampling techniques of these societies are different and each has its proponents, but in the end each aims to collect and pay the public performance fees to the copyright owners who have signed agreements with it.

As noted, the actual fee paid to the publisher and to the writer for the single performance of a song is determined by each of the performing rights organizations through an intricate weighting formula and depends on factors such as whether a radio broadcast is AM or FM, network or local, and on the aggregate number of times the song is performed. A number-one single on the Billboard Hot 100 would generate roughly between $70,000 and $90,000 in performing rights royalties, depending on how long the song retained its popularity. This income would be split between the publisher and the songwriter.[4] A local hit might not even turn up in the samples, and even though it was publicly performed, the songwriter might receive no royalties. The royalties that are paid for performances are split between the publisher and songwriter according to their agreement, and the performing rights society sends each a check for its respective share.

RIGHTS IN THE SOUND RECORDING

Like the song, the sound recording can have a number of personalities who have a role in creating it. The most prominent are the name-artist or name-group who are the major musicians on the recording. The Commodores, Fleetwood Mac, and George Benson are well-known name artists. Their record contract generally provides that they are *employed* by the record company to record and, as employees for hire, they do not become owners of the sound recording. Their rights in an album are determined by the contract they have entered with the producer or record company and, as discussed below, their interest primarily takes the form of a right to receive royalties on albums sold.

In addition to the royalty artists, session or studio musicians may be involved in the recording. The session payment rate and other compensation are largely governed by union wage scale agreements between the American Federation of Musicians (for instrumentalists), the American Federation of Television and Radio Artists (for vocalists), and the major record companies.

The other significant income from the sound recording belongs to the record company and to the independent producer, if there is one. Here practice varies widely. Often an independent producer will discover talent, enter a recording contract with the performer, cut a master, and end up owning the sound recording. He or she then may sell the master to a major label for a flat sum or for a percentage of sales; sometimes the independent producer may assign the contract with the performer to the record company. Regardless of how it is handled, the rights will conform to whatever agreement the independent producer and record company reach, which is typically set out in a written contract. The royalty rate for an independent producer ranges from 2 to 5 percent of the retail sales price for each unit sold.

PERFORMER INCOME FROM PHONORECORD SALES

The recording agreement that a rock band, for example, typically signs on its first record deal may pay royalties of between 5 and 10 percent of the retail sales price, less an allowance for returns and a deduction for packaging. Generally, royalties to the recording artist for record club sales and foreign sales are one-half the standard retail rate, and no artist royalties are payable for promotional copies.

Note that the royalties payable to a recording artist under the record contract are entirely separate from the royalties a songwriter receives from use of a song. Bob Dylan receives both types of royalties on albums he records, as do other individuals who are both songwriters and performers.

The major disadvantage of the standard recording contract from the musician's point of view is that the contract is structured so that unless he gets a cash advance from the record company, the musician receives no money for the recording (other than union scale) until he has accumulated enough royalties to offset all the recording costs for the album. These costs include studio time, engineering, session musician fees, record producer, and all the other expenses that went into producing the master.

Since an estimated 70–80 percent of the albums released each year are financial losers, in most cases the recording artist never sees a royalty check. The record company absorbs the non-recouped recording costs or charges them against royalties on future albums by the performer. This charging costs against future albums is called cross-collateralization and can result in a performer receiving no royalties on even a gold or platinum album if his earlier album sales failed to recoup their costs. Although a performer may never see any royalties on the record sales, if the performer has rights in the songs performed, he or she may receive songwriter or publisher royalties.

RECORD COMPANY INCOME FROM PHONORECORD SALES

The record company, as owner of the sound recording of the performance, has the exclusive right to make phonorecords of the sound recording and to sell them.[5] Unless it owns the copyright in the songs, however, it must pay songwriter royalties for the mechanical use of the songs. It also may have a contractual obligation to pay royalties to the performers on the record and to the producer. The record company, of course, also must pay the costs of manufacture, promotions, and distribution.

Record companies generally sell records to wholesale distributors for approximately one-half list price. The distributor takes a mark-up of 10 to 30 percent, and the retailer again marks the record up before the consumer takes it out of the store. Assuming that a record lists for $9.98 and it is sold in a discount store for $7.98, that $7.98 will be broken down roughly as follows:

Retailer	$1.90
Wholesale Distributor	1.40
Packaging and Shipping	.50
Advertising and Promotion	.30
Record Company Administration	.64
Pressing and Manufacture	.72
Record Company Profit	1.30
Song Publisher	.20
Songwriter(s)	.20
Artist (+ Producer)	.82
Total	$7.98[6]

RECORD COMPANY AND PERFORMER INCOME FROM PUBLIC PERFORMANCE OF SOUND RECORDINGS

It is important to point out that people with rights in the sound recording are not entitled to any fees for a radio or TV broadcast, because there is no exclusive right of public performance in a sound recording (see chapter

1, "Limitations on Exclusive Rights in Sound Recordings").[7] At present, radio airplay creates no income for the performer or the record company. To them, radio airplay is useful only as advertising for the retail sale of the record or to draw people to concerts. Congress is considering amending the Copyright Act to provide for royalties on the performance of sound recordings.[8] If the law is amended, these royalties would probably be divided on some basis between the performing artist and the record company. In many European countries royalties are paid on the performances of copyrighted sound recordings.

MOVIE SOUND TRACKS

One other area that deserves mention is the use of music in sound tracks for movies and television. When a film producer arranges to obtain a piece of music for a movie, he or she has two choices: either hire or commission someone to write original music; or arrange with the owner of a previously composed musical composition to use that composition in the sound track. The former situation generally involves an employee-for-hire or specially ordered or commissioned agreement, while the latter requires obtaining synchronization and performance licenses.

When the music is created for the film in a work made for hire situation, the film producer generally enters a written agreement with the composer by which the composer agrees to write the music score for a fee, and the film producer or film company becomes the owner of the music score.[9] When the producer obtains the copyright for the work once it is created, he or she automatically obtains each of the component portions of the copyright, including sychronization and performance rights.

When the film producer decides to use previously copyrighted music for the movie, he or she must obtain a synchronization and performance license from the copyright owner. A synchronization license is the right to record the music with the action of the motion picture. In addition to obtaining this right, a movie producer must obtain the right to publicly perform the synchronized music during the exhibition of the film in other media. Arrangements must be made to secure both rights.[10] Television is a different situation. The performing rights societies grant blanket performance licenses to television broadcasters for fees, and the television producer must secure only the synchronization rights. Litigation is pending, however, that may force television producers to acquire performance rights as well.

When using music with video cassettes and video disks, a separate license would have to be negotiated with the publisher, unless this right already had been obtained. Fees to be paid for such use often include a flat fee to be paid when the deal is made as well as a number of cents (e.g., .5 to .7) per title, per unit sold, or a percentage of retail or wholesale divided among the owners of the music on the video cassettes or video disks.

Many music publishers utilize the services of the Harry Fox Agency in licensing synchronization and performance rights in musical compositions for motion picture use. If the Harry Fox Agency (or another licensing agency) does not handle the particular musical composition in which the producer is interested, the film producer must go directly to the copyright owner and negotiate a license.

Generally, of course, a producer seeks broad synchronization and performance licenses in order to permit the use of the music with the film in an unlimited way—for example, showing the film worldwide in theaters, on television, and in video cassettes. The owner of the musical composition, by contrast, may want to limit the license. For example, the copyright owner may try to restrict the license to the United States and Canada, thus requiring the film producer to obtain separate licenses for foreign countries. The music owner also may seek to create separate license requirements for pay and cable television and home video cassettes and may try to limit the duration of the license. At this time most publishers are agreeing to negotiate royalties for cassettes for a set period of time (e.g., two years) after initial distribution of the cassette.

The recording artist who performs the musical composition for the movie sound track also will have to focus on what rights, if any, he or she will have in album sales of the sound track, above and beyond the money received for performing the songs in connection with the making of the movie.

There are special problems in copyrights of component parts of a motion picture. Generally the Copyright Office takes the position that a music sound track is an integral portion of the whole film and cannot be segregated for a separate copyright.[11] Release of the film prior to the independent publication and registration of the songs and sound recording will usually result in the refusal of the Copyright Office to allow a separate registration of the song or sound recording, unless a separate copyright notice for that part has been placed on the film. Prior commercial release and registration of the musical sound track in album form is even better. This is one reason that you often will find movie sound track albums in the record stores before the film is premiered.

TYPICAL DIVISION OF MUSIC INCOME

Rights of	*Performance*	*Phonorecords*
	By radio or TV broadcast, live concerts, and juke boxes	Retail sales of records and tapes
Publisher	Collects its share of royalties directly through a performing rights society (ASCAP, BMI, or SESAC), with songwriter and publisher generally dividing performance royalties 50/50	Collects mechanical use royalties per record sold by record company, and then splits royalty with songwriter
Songwriter	Collects his or her half of royalties directly through performing rights society (ASCAP, BMI, or SESAC) for performances	Collects half of mechanical use royalties paid to publisher
Record Company	Collects no royalties when its record is played over the air, even though it is a public performance of the sound recording	Collects wholesale price of record but must pay manufacturing costs and may have to pay royalties on sales to recording artist and independent producer and to publisher on the mechanical use
Recording Artist	Collects no royalties when record is broadcast; however, Congress is considering amending the Copyright Act to provide for performance royalties	Is paid a royalty by record company of generally between 5 and 10 percent of the retail price for records sold, but all recording costs must be recouped before actually receives cash
Independent Producer	Same as for recording artist	Is paid a royalty by record company of between 2 and 5 percent of the retail price for records sold but with no recoupment

Infringement

CHAPTER **FIVE**

The primary benefit provided by the Copyright Act is the exclusive privilege to commercially exploit the rights recognized in copyright ownership. This benefit is protected by the provisions of the Act that give the copyright owner the right to sue those who invade this privilege by bringing an infringement action against them. The 1976 Copyright Act, unlike the old copyright law, states exactly what constitutes an infringement.[1] An infringement occurs when any of the copyright owner's exclusive rights are violated,[2] or when unauthorized copies or phonorecords are imported.[3] As noted earlier, the five fundamental rights given to a copyright owner—the exclusive rights of reproduction, adaptation, publication, performance, and display—comprise the so-called bundle of rights that is a copyright. A single act of infringement may violate a number of these rights at once—as when a publisher, without permission, reproduces, adapts, and sells copies of a person's copyrighted work as part of a publishing venture.[4] Infringement also takes place when any one of the rights is violated—as when the publisher only reproduces copies but never sells them. This is still infringement.

INFRINGEMENT OF MUSICAL WORKS AND SOUND RECORDINGS

Music is typically fixed in a tangible medium of expression by being reduced to sheet music or by being embodied in tapes or phonograph records. Once your music is reduced to musical notation, you then have the bundle of rights in that sheet music. No one may reproduce, adapt, publish, or perform the music without your permission. (The right to public display also applies to musical works, but it is important primarily with regard to pictorial, graphic, and sculptural works.)[5]

The most patent example of infringing sheet music occurs when someone photocopies your work and sells the copies. This violates both your right to reproduce the music and to publish it; thus, it constitutes infringement. Your right of adaptation is violated when someone writes an arrangement of your song and publishes it without your permission.

The other typical way that musical works are fixed is when they are embodied in a phonorecord. As discussed earlier, the owner of a copyright in a sound recording (typically, a record company) has the right to reproduce the sound recording in phonorecords, to prepare derivative works based on the copyrighted sound recording, and to distribute phonorecords of the sound recording to the public.[6]

The most obvious example of infringement of a sound recording (whether fixed on a phonograph record or tape) occurs when someone takes the sound recording, puts it on tape, and makes and sells phonorecords from that tape. This violates both your right to reproduce and your right to distribute. The right to prepare derivative works is violated when the actual sounds fixed in the sound recording are taken, rearranged or revised, and re-fixed on a phonorecord or tape.[7] This problem is usually not a significant one, since most people elect to make their own sound recording under a compulsory or negotiated mechanical license.[8]

In music, numerous infringement questions arise when there is a partial copying in a new song of a previously published or recorded song. A common myth in the music field is that in composing a song, a writer can graft four bars from a copyrighted song, and this is a fair use[9] for which he or she cannot be sued. The fact is that there is no absolute and precise measure of what pattern of notes or lyrics can be incorporated into a new song without infringing the old song. We all recognize that standard chord progressions (I, IV, V being the classic example) and stock phrases ("I'm still in love with you") pervade countless musical compositions. And it is obvious no one can claim the exclusive right to either of these.

EVEN A BEATLE HAS INFRINGED

Normally, to show infringement the copyright owner must show that the infringer copied his or her copyrighted work. The owner must show that the infringer had access to the copyrighted work, and that the infringer made a substantial taking from the copyrighted work.[10] The taking need not be conscious—a song can be subconsciously copied.[11]

George Harrison found this out the hard way. In a recent case he was found to have infringed the song "He's So Fine," recorded in 1962 by the Chiffons, with his 1970 hit "My Sweet Lord."

"He's So Fine" consists essentially of four repetitions of a very short basic musical phrase, "sol-mi-re" (or G, E, D on the treble clef, which we will call motif A):

followed by four repetitions of another short basic musical phrase, "sol-la-do-la-do" (or G, A, C, A, C on the treble clef, which we will call motif B):

While neither of these musical phrases is in itself novel ("He's So Fine" consists of the first phrase repeated four times, followed by the second musical phrase repeated four times), the phrases and their repetitions when taken together formed a highly unique pattern.[12] "My Sweet Lord" uses the same motif A (modified to suit the words) four times, followed by motif B, repeated three times, not four (as did "He's So Fine"). Additionally, "My Sweet Lord" used a traditional passage (bridge), with a grace note identical to one in "He's So Fine." Furthermore, the harmonies of both songs are identical. Thus the music of "He's So Fine" and "My Sweet Lord" is virtually the same.[13] Although the lyrics were entirely dissimilar both literally and conceptually (the Chiffons longed for the love of a man; Harrison chanted his praise of God), the similarity of the music constituted a substantial taking.

How did Harrison have access to "He's So Fine"? The Chiffons' "He's So Fine" (remember "dulang, dulang,

dulang"?) was No. 1 on the Billboard charts; and in England it was one of the top hits for seven weeks in 1963.[14] (Ironically, on June 1, 1963, "He's So Fine" made No. 12 on the British charts, while the Beatles occupied the No. 1 spot.)[15] From these facts the court inferred Harrison had access. Harrison subconsciously recreated "He's So Fine" by writing "My Sweet Lord."[16] This was still an infringement. Note that Harrison did not infringe the Chiffons' sound recording, but infringed the underlying musical work. The owner of the underlying musical work, Bright Tunes Music Corporation, brought the suit. As we discussed above, in a music publishing contract the songwriter typically will grant legal title to the copyright in exchange for a percentage of the music publisher's income from the song.

WHO MAY SUE FOR INFRINGEMENT

Only the legal or beneficial owner of an exclusive right under copyright may sue for infringement of that right.[17] Since copyright is actually a "bundle of rights" that can be divided and sold separately, a songwriter often will grant to a publishing company his or her right to exploit the musical work and to receive royalties therefrom, and the songwriter and publishing company will then share those royalties. At that point, although the songwriter is no longer the legal owner of the right, he or she remains the beneficial owner (that is, he or she still receives benefits from it—his or her share of the royalties that the publisher collects). If someone is infringing the copyright, both the publishing company (legal owner) and the songwriter (beneficial owner) may sue the infringer.

As noted earlier, no legal action may be instituted until registration of the copyright claim has been filed with the Register of Copyrights.[18] Nevertheless, a copyright owner whose work is infringed before registration is entitled, upon subsequent registration, to the relief ordinarily available in infringement cases: an injunction on terms the court considers fair, and his or her proven actual damages plus any profits made by the infringer.[19]

As an incentive for registration of copyrighted works, the Copyright Act denies any award of statutory damages or attorney's fees for copyright infringement occurring prior to the registration of the work,[20] except in the case of an infringement of a published work that has been registered within a grace period of three months after its publication.[21] This three-month grace period anticipates the case of a suddenly popular work that may be infringed almost as soon as it is published and before the copyright owner has had a reasonable opportunity to register the claim. Thus, if an album with the proper notice is released on January 1, 1984, and zooms to the top of the charts, someone may immediately infringe the sound recording embodied in the album by reproducing it on tapes. Even though sound recording embodied in the album is not immediately registered under Form SR, as long as it is registered by March 31, 1984 (within three months of publication), the holder of the sound recording copyright may sue for infringement during the period commencing with January 1, 1984, and demand statutory damages and attorneys' fees.

With respect to unpublished works there is no three-month grace period.[22] Because statutory damages are often the only monetary relief available, and few attorneys will want to bring an infringement action without the prospect of court-awarded attorney's fees, this provision tends to deprive the songwriter of unpublished songs of any remedies against an infringer of his or her unpublished work. Therefore, the safest course is to register unpublished songs immediately, and to register published songs as soon as possible, but no later than three months after the initial publication.

IMITATIONS OF SOUNDS NOT AN INFRINGEMENT

Remember that the statutory protection for sound recordings extends only to the particular sounds of which the recording consists. Thus, infringement takes place whenever all or any substantial portion of the actual sounds that make up a copyrighted sound recording are reproduced in phonorecords by any method,[23] or by reproducing them in the sound-track or audio portion of a motion picture or videotape without the copyright owner's permission.[24]

Mere imitation of a recorded performance by means of a separate, independent sound recording does not constitute a copyright infringement, even when a performer sets out to simulate another's performance as exactly as possible.[25] This is sometimes a troubling problem with so-called greatest hits packages that consist of rerecordings of hit singles by performers other than the original hit artist. Under the Copyright Act this recording may be done, providing a compulsory or negotiated mechanical license is obtained from the owner of the copyright in the underlying songs.[26] Permission of the original performer or record company is not required unless they happen to have right in the songs. The compulsory mechanical license under the Act provides for a standard royalty fee.[27] With a negotiated license the fee, if there is one, is set by the parties and often it is exactly the so-called "statutory" rate. A greatest hits album could encounter legal problems, however, even if there is no infringement under the Copyright Act. Most states have laws prohibiting the passing off of goods as another's, and the packaging and advertising of the product must not deceive the consumer concerning the performance of the work.[28] It must be made clear on the face of the imitating product that the recording is not the original, but rather is an imitation.

INFRINGEMENT OF THE COMPULSORY MECHANICAL LICENSE

While the Copyright Act has a compulsory license provision that permits anyone complying with the provision to record another's songs,[29] there is no compulsory licensing of sound recordings.[30] Unauthorized duplication of a sound recording is an infringement.[31] Thus, one may not record albums on cassettes and sell them commercially without the permission of the owner of the copyright in the sound recording and without having obtained a mechanical license from the owner of the song. One can, however, produce a new recording of the songs from the album by obtaining a negotiated or compulsory mechanical license.

INJUNCTION

A copyright owner whose rights are being infringed often needs immediate action by the court to stop an infringement. For example, an infringer might be importing unauthorized copies of an album that are taking away from the album's domestic sales. The copyright owner may stop the importation by petitioning the court to issue an injunction[32]—that is, a court order prohibiting importation. Injunctions also may be issued to prevent infringement.[33] Thus, if the copyright owner learns of the importation scheme before it actually occurs, he or she may get an injunction to forbid it before it happens.[34] Injunctions under the copyright law are enforceable throughout the United States,[35] not just in the state where they are obtained.

IMPOUNDING AND DESTRUCTION OF INFRINGING ARTICLES

As soon as an infringement suit is filed, the court may order the impounding of the copies or phonorecords allegedly violating the copyright laws, as well as the articles used to reproduce the copies or phonorecords.[36] Thus, if an infringer is making records from a tape of an illicitly recorded live performance, the records being produced from the tape, the tape itself, and the manufacturing equipment may be confiscated under court order.[37] If infringement is found upon completion of the suit, the court may dispose of both the infringing copies or phonorecords and the articles used in the reproduction, as the court sees fit. The infringing articles could be sold, delivered to the rightful copyright owner, or destroyed.[38]

DAMAGES AND PROFITS

Proving the amount of damages caused to a copyright owner is often an impossible task. Recognizing this, the Copyright Act, as noted earlier, sets out statutory damages[39] (that is, the law itself sets out the amount to be awarded regardless of proof of damages).[40] If, however, the copyright owner can prove the amount of damages and the profits from the infringement by the infringer, the copyright owner may recover both these amounts.[41] The copyright owner cannot, however, recover both statutory damages and non-statutory damages. He or she must choose between the two.[42] The obvious choice is the one potentially providing more money. The decision may be made by the copyright owner at any time before the court makes its final judgment.[43]

In general, when a copyright owner elects statutory damages, the court must award between $250 and $10,000.[44] This covers the situation when a single infringer infringes a single work, regardless of how many acts of infringements were involved.[45] Thus, if one person makes 1,000 illegal tapes of a sound recording, this is one infringement—not 1,000 infringements.[46] Also, if more than one person infringes a work, the parties are jointly liable, but the award is not multiplied. Thus, if two people simultaneously infringe the sound recording, they are liable in the range of $250 to $10,000, not $500 to $20,000.

When separate works are involved, however, statutory damages are awarded for each infringement. For example, if a defendant has copied and sold three separate copyrighted songs fixed in sheet music, the copyright owner is entitled to statutory damages of at least $750, and may be awarded up to $30,000.[47] On the other hand, if the song were in a songbook (a compilation), and the defendant copied the songbook, this would be a single act of infringement,[48] even if the songbook contained 100 songs.

In exceptional cases maximum statutory damages may be raised or minimum damage awards may be reduced.[49] If the infringer has *willfully* (that is, purposefully) infringed a copyright, the court may raise the recovery from the non-willful $10,000 limit to $50,000. On the other hand, statutory damages may be reduced from $250 to not less than $100 if the infringement was *innocent* (that is, the infringer was unaware of the infringement).[50] In addition, in certain cases when the infringer believed his or her infringement was a fair use, the award of statutory damages is disallowed.[51] This fair use exception, however, only covers non-profit institutions and their employees.[52] Thus, even if an infringer had a good faith belief that the infringement was an example of fair use, he or she is still liable for infringement unless an employee of a non-profit institution.

COURT COSTS AND ATTORNEY'S FEES

The court may award both court costs and attorney's fees to the party or parties prevailing in the suit.[53] The courts will be more likely to award attorney's fees when they find willful infringement.[54]

CRIMINAL PENALTIES

Willful infringers who infringe for commercial advantage or private financial gain are subject to up to a $10,000 fine and one year in jail.[55] Special penalties, however, apply when the criminally infringed work is a sound recording.[56] Any person who willfully infringes a copyright in a sound recording for commercial advantage can be fined up to $25,000 and imprisoned for one year. For any subsequent offense a person can be fined up to $50,000 and imprisoned for two years.[57] The court can also order the infringing copies and the equipment used to produce them to be forfeited and destroyed.[58] Fines up to $2,500 are authorized for knowingly placing fraudulent copyright notice or importing or distributing copies with fraudulent copyright notices.[59] The same fines are authorized for removal or alteration of a copyright notice,[60] or making a false representation in registering a copyright.[61]

Congress recently stiffened criminal penalties for trafficking in counterfeit labels for phonorecords and criminal infringement of sound recordings. These infringers can be fined up to $250,000 and imprisoned for up to five years.

STATUTE OF LIMITATIONS

No criminal or civil action may be brought under the Copyright Act unless it is filed within three years of the offending act.[62] It is imperative, therefore, that legal help be sought as soon as you suspect your copyright rights have been violated.

JUKE BOX COMPULSORY LICENSE

Operators of coin-operated phonorecord players (juke boxes) must now obtain a compulsory license in order to avoid infringement when playing phonorecords contained in the juke box.[63] The license is obtained by filing an application with the Copyright Office and paying a $25 fee.[64] The Copyright Office then issues a certificate to the juke box operator that must be put on the juke box where it can be read.[65] In addition to civil suits for infringement,[66] any person who makes a false statement on the application, alters the juke box certificate, or purposely puts the certificate on a juke box it does not cover may be criminally liable for a fine up to $2,500.[67]

In order to share in the juke box royalties generated during the previous year, the copyright owner must file a claim with the Copyright Royalty Tribunal during the month of January.[68] Writers associated with performing rights societies, such as ASCAP, BMI, and SESAC, will have them make claims and collect royalties on their behalf.[69]

UNAUTHORIZED IMPORTATION

Often a copyright holder in a sound recording will license domestic and foreign record distribution separately. The unauthorized importation of copies or phonorecords acquired outside the United States is an infringement, as it violates the copyright owner's exclusive right to distribute copies or phonorecords.

Section 602 of the Copyright Act (unauthorized importation)[70] distinguishes two separate situations: importation of pirated articles;[71] and unauthorized importation of copies of phonorecords that were lawfully made.[72] This distinction is important, as the law treats these two situations differently.[73]

Pirated copies of phonorecords are those made without the copyright owner's authorization. Thus, if Warner Bros. Records licenses a British record company to make and distribute George Benson's *Weekend in LA* album in Great Britain, the mere fact the phonorecord is distributed in England does not allow the licensee or anyone else in England to make tapes of the phonorecord and bring them into the United States. Also, even though one might purchase an authorized phonorecord in Britain, it is still an infringement to bring that phonorecord into the United States, as Warner Bros. retains the exclusive right to distribute in the United States.[74]

Does this mean if you buy *Weekend in LA* in London and go through customs in San Francisco, that the Bureau of Customs will confiscate it? No. The Copyright Act sets out an exception that if the phonorecord is for your private use (i.e., not for distribution), and you have only one copy, you may lawfully bring it into this country.[75]

What if you have an overseas guest whose baggage is crammed full of phonorecords acquired overseas? Again, the phonorecords are not subject to Customs confiscation, as long as they form part of the traveler's baggage.[76] The Customs people, may, however, take note of the contents[77] or confiscate them if there is an injunction ordering so.[78]

On the other hand, assume you are at Customs with a suitcase full of pirated *Weekend in LA* tapes. The tapes, like other materials that violate Customs revenue laws, are subject to seizure and forfeiture.[79] Additionally, you would be subject to both criminal and civil penalties. Even if it were legal in Britain to record *Weekend in LA* on tapes, it is illegal to bring these tapes into the United States.

AVOIDING INFRINGEMENT

How can you avoid infringing other songs when you compose songs? First, avoid grafting (that is, a direct taking note for note, word for word, or beat for beat). If you like a particular riff or phrase, integrate it into a composition that adds something that distinguishes it from the previous song. When George Harrison wrote "My Sweet Lord," his changes from "He's So Fine" were not sufficient to distinguish it. Of course, if you like a complete song and wish to record it (with or without minor changes), you must get either a negotiated or compulsory mechanical license to do so.[80] If you intend to publish your own arrangement of the song, you must get permission from the copyright holder since he or she has the right to prepare derivative works[81] and an arrangement is a derivative work.[82]

Use your own style. If you want to adopt part of a Bee Gees song, try not to make the recording sound like the Bee Gees (e.g., avoid lavish falsetto harmonies). When and if there is an infringement trial, the judge or jury will necessarily listen to both recordings to compare them. The closer the sound, the more likely the finding of an infringement.[83] If you are performing an original song you wrote, however, you are free to sound as much like the Bee Gees as you like.

As previously discussed, you also are free to take from songs in the public domain—that is, songs which were not copyrighted, or whose copyright has expired. A good example of this is Barry Manilow's 1973 hit "Could It Be Magic." The song was inspired by Frederic Chopin's "Prelude in C Minor." Chopin's song, however, was written in the nineteenth century and was never subject to United States copyright laws—and even if it had been, the copyright would have expired. Thus, Manilow was free to put the music to new lyrics. Although Arista Records now holds the copyright to the sound recording "Could It Be Magic," and Manilow's publishing company holds the copyright in the musical work, the music from Chopin's "Prelude in C Minor" remains in the public domain, and is free for you to use.

This result occurs because "Could It Be Magic" is a *derivative work*[84]—that is, a work based on a pre-existing work (in this case, Chopin's "Prelude in C Minor"). The copyright in a derivative work extends only to the material contributed by the author of the derivative work, as distinguished from the pre-existing material employed in the work.[85] Copyright in a derivative work does not give any exclusive right in the pre-existing work, nor does it affect the copyright in the preexisting work.[86] Thus, Chopin's "Prelude in C Minor" remains in the public domain. You are free to adapt it. Do not use Manilow's lyrics or his arrangement, however, because they were his original contribution to the musical work "Could It Be Magic," and are therefore protected by copyright as original works.

FAIR USE

As discussed in chapter 1, the doctrine of fair use[87] limits the exclusive rights of the copyright holder. This doctrine arises when there has been a copying, but the copying is fair. As discussed, courts will consider four criteria to measure a fair use. The central question is the effect of the use on the potential sales of the original work.[88] The second most important question is the amount of the copyrighted portion used.[89]

Thus, if in the middle of a song you want to break into a riff from David Bowie and John Lennon's "Fame," you could probably play a few bars without infringing. This insignificant taking, though it might make "Fame" pop into a listener's mind, would most likely not affect sales of the sound recording of "Fame" or the "Fame" sheet music. Also, the taking would not be significant in relation to the entire work "Fame."

On the other hand, if you made an almost exact copy of "Fame" and merely changed the lyrics, you would likely be an infringer, as George Harrison was with "My Sweet Lord." If your song sounds exactly like "Fame," people may buy phonorecords or sheet music of your song instead of "Fame"; thus, the potential sales are diminished. Also, your taking would be a substantial one.

RECORD REVIEWS

The policy underlying fair use is to encourage criticism, research, and the flow of ideas. Thus, *Rolling Stone* magazine may print record album reviews that make short, illustrative quotations without the copyright owner's permission. One can imagine that it would be impossible to review Randy Newman's "Short People" without copying part of the lyrics. This is a fair use for at least two reasons: the amount taken is insignificant; and the potential for sales of "Short People" is not diminished. If anything, the market is improved. Obviously, people wishing to buy "Short People" in order to perform it could not perform it based on the record review. Also, the use of the lyrics is acceptable because the lyrics are not being used in a song, but in criticism. *Rolling Stone* would infringe, however, if it reproduced the sheet music in its entirety—people wanting the song for musical purposes could buy *Rolling Stone* instead of the album or sheet music.[90]

Rather than relying solely on the fair use exemption, the better practice is to obtain permission of the copyright owner (usually the song publisher) before quoting lyrics in a review. Most publishers give this permission freely and require only that a proper copyright notice be printed and the words "used by permission" be utilized in the review.

Appendix

FORM PA

UNITED STATES COPYRIGHT OFFICE
LIBRARY OF CONGRESS
WASHINGTON, D.C. 20559

APPLICATION FOR COPYRIGHT REGISTRATION

for a Work of the Performing Arts

HOW TO APPLY FOR COPYRIGHT REGISTRATION:

- ***First:*** Read the information on this page to make sure Form PA is the correct application for your work.
- ***Second:*** Open out the form by pulling this page to the left. Read through the detailed instructions before starting to complete the form.
- ***Third:*** Complete spaces 1-4 of the application, then turn the entire form over and, after reading the instructions for spaces 5-9, complete the rest of your application. Use typewriter or print in dark ink. Be sure to sign the form at space 8.
- ***Fourth:*** Detach your completed application from these instructions and send it with the necessary deposit of the work (see below) to: Register of Copyrights, Library of Congress, Washington, D.C. 20559. Unless you have a Deposit Account in the Copyright Office, your application and deposit must be accompanied by a check or money order for $10, payable to: *Register of Copyrights.*

WHEN TO USE FORM PA: Form PA is the appropriate application to use for copyright registration covering works of the performing arts. Both published and unpublished works can be registered on Form PA.

WHAT IS A "WORK OF THE PERFORMING ARTS"? This category includes works prepared for the purpose of being "performed" directly before an audience or indirectly "by means of any device or process." Examples of works of the performing arts are: (1) musical works, including any accompanying words; (2) dramatic works, including any accompanying music; (3) pantomimes and choreographic works; and (4) motion pictures and other audiovisual works. **Note:** This category does not include sound recordings, which should be registered on Form SR. For more information about copyright in sound recordings, see the reverse side of this sheet.

DEPOSIT TO ACCOMPANY APPLICATION: An application for copyright registration must be accompanied by a deposit representing the entire work for which registration is to be made. The following are the general deposit requirements as set forth in the statute:

Unpublished work: Deposit one complete copy or phonorecord.

Published work: Deposit two complete copies or phonorecords of the best edition.

Work first published outside the United States: Deposit one complete copy or phonorecord of the first foreign edition.

Contribution to a collective work: Deposit one complete copy or phonorecord of the best edition of the collective work.

These general deposit requirements may vary in particular situations. For further information about the specific deposit requirements for particular types of works of the performing arts, see the reverse side of this sheet. For general information about copyright deposit, write to the Copyright Office.

THE COPYRIGHT NOTICE: For published works, the law provides that a copyright notice in a specified form "shall be placed on all publicly distributed copies from which the work can be visually perceived." Use of the copyright notice is the responsibility of the copyright owner and does not require advance permission from the Copyright Office. The required form of the notice for copies generally consists of three elements: (1) the symbol "©", or the word "Copyright", or the abbreviation "Copr."; (2) the year of first publication; and (3) the name of the owner of copyright. For example: "© 1978 Alexander Hollenius". The notice is to be affixed to the copies "in such manner and location as to give reasonable notice of the claim of copyright." Unlike the law in effect before 1978, the new copyright statute provides procedures for correcting errors in the copyright notice, and even for curing the omission of the notice. However, a failure to comply with the notice requirements may still result in the loss of some copyright protection and, unless corrected within five years, in the complete loss of copyright. For further information about the copyright notice, see the reverse side of this sheet. For additional information concerning the copyright notice and the procedures for correcting errors or omissions, write to the Copyright Office.

DURATION OF COPYRIGHT: For works that were created after the effective date of the new statute (January 1, 1978), the basic copyright term will be the life of the author and fifty years after the author's death. For works made for hire, and for certain anonymous and pseudonymous works, the duration of copyright will be 75 years from publication or 100 years from creation, whichever is shorter. These same terms of copyright will generally apply to works that had been created before 1978 but had not been published or copyrighted before that date. For further information about the duration of copyright, including the terms of copyrights already in existence before 1978, write for Circular R15a.

HOW TO FILL OUT FORM PA

Specific Instructions for Spaces 1-4

- The line-by-line instructions on this page are keyed to the spaces on the first page of Form PA, printed opposite.
- Please read through these instructions before you start filling out your application, and refer to the specific instructions for each space as you go along.

SPACE 1: TITLE

• ***Title of this Work:*** Every work submitted for copyright registration must be given a title that is capable of identifying that particular work. If the copies or phonorecords of the work bear a title (or an identifying phrase that could serve as a title), transcribe its wording completely and exactly on the application. Remember that indexing of the registration and future identification of the work will depend on the information you give here.

If the work you are registering is an entire "collective work" (such as a collection of plays or songs), give the over-all title of the collection. If you are registering one or more individual contributions to a collective work, give the title of each contribution, followed by the title of the collection. Example: " 'A Song for Elinda' in *Old and New Ballads for Old and New People*."

• ***Nature of this Work:*** Briefly describe the general nature or character of the work being registered for copyright. Examples: "Music"; "Song Lyrics"; "Words and Music"; "Drama"; "Musical Play", "Choreography"; "Pantomime"; "Motion Picture"; "Audiovisual Work".

• ***Previous or Alternative Titles:*** Complete this space if there are any additional titles for the work under which someone searching for the registration might be likely to look, or under which a document pertaining to the work might be recorded.

SPACE 2: AUTHORS

• ***General Instructions:*** First decide, after reading these instructions, who are the "authors" of this work for copyright purposes. Then, unless the work is a "collective work" (see below), give the requested information about every "author" who contributed any appreciable amount of copyrightable matter to this version of the work. If you need further space, use the attached Continuation Sheet and, if necessary, request additional Continuation Sheets (Form PA/CON).

• ***Who is the "Author"?*** Unless the work was "made for hire," the individual who actually created the work is its "author." In the case of a work made for hire, the statute provides that "the employer or other person for whom the work was prepared is considered the author."

• ***What is a "Work Made for Hire"?*** A "work made for hire" is defined as: (1) "a work prepared by an employee within the scope of his or her employment"; or (2) "a work specially ordered or commissioned" for certain uses specified in the statute, but only if there is a written agreement to consider it a "work made for hire."

• ***Collective Work:*** In the case of a collective work, such as a song book or a collection of plays, it is sufficient to give information about the author of the collective work as a whole.

• ***Author's Identity Not Revealed:*** If an author's contribution is "anonymous" or "pseudonymous," it is not necessary to give the name and dates for that author. However, the citizenship or domicile of the author **must** be given in all cases, and information about the nature of that author's contribution to the work should be included.

• ***Name of Author:*** The fullest form of the author's name should be given. If you have checked "Yes" to indicate that the work was "made for hire," give the full legal name of the employer (or other person for whom the work was prepared). You may also include the name of the employee (for example: "Music Makers Publishing Co., employer for hire of Lila Crane"). If the work is "anonymous" you may: (1) leave the line blank, or (2) state "Anonymous" in the line, or (3) reveal the author's identity. If the work is "pseudonymous" you may (1) leave the line blank, or (2) give the pseudonym and identify it as such (for example: "Huntley Haverstock, pseudonym"), or (3) reveal the author's name, making clear which is the real name and which is the pseudonym (for example, "Judith Barton, whose pseudonym is Madeleine Elster").

• ***Dates of Birth and Death:*** If the author is dead, the statute requires that the year of death be included in the application unless the work is anonymous or pseudonymous. The author's birth date is optional, but is useful as a form of identification. Leave this space blank if the author's contribution was a "work made for hire."

• ***"Anonymous" or "Pseudonymous" Work:*** An author's contribution to a work is "anonymous" if that author is not identified on the copies or phonorecords of the work. An author's contribution to a work is "pseudonymous" if that author is identified on the copies or phonorecords under a fictitious name.

• ***Author's Nationality or Domicile:*** Give the country of which the author is a citizen, or the country in which the author is domiciled. The statute requires that either nationality or domicile be given in all cases.

• ***Nature of Authorship:*** After the words "Author of" give a brief general statement of the nature of this particular author's contribution to the work. Examples: "Words"; "Co-Author of Music"; "Words and Music"; "Arrangement"; "Co-Author of Book and Lyrics"; "Dramatization"; "Entire Work"; "Compilation and English Translation"; "Editorial Revisions".

SPACE 3: CREATION AND PUBLICATION

• ***General Instructions:*** Do not confuse "creation" with "publication." Every application for copyright registration must state "the year in which creation of the work was completed." Give the date and nation of first publication only if the work has been published.

• ***Creation:*** Under the statute, a work is "created" when it is fixed in a copy or phonorecord for the first time. Where a work has been prepared over a period of time, the part of the work existing in fixed form on a particular date constitutes the created work on that date. The date you give here should be the year in which the author completed the particular version for which registration is now being sought, even if other versions exist or if further changes or additions are planned.

• ***Publication:*** The statute defines "publication" as "the distribution of copies or phonorecords of a work to the public by sale or other transfer of ownership, or by rental, lease, or lending"; a work is also "published" if there has been an "offering to distribute copies or phonorecords to a group of persons for purposes of further distribution, public performance, or public display." Give the full date (month, day, year) when, and the country where, publication first occurred. If first publication took place simultaneously in the United States and other countries, it is sufficient to state "U.S.A."

SPACE 4: CLAIMANT(S)

• ***Name(s) and Address(es) of Copyright Claimant(s):*** Give the name(s) and address(es) of the copyright claimant(s) in this work. The statute provides that copyright in a work belongs initially to the author of the work (including, in the case of a work made for hire, the employer or other person for whom the work was prepared). The copyright claimant is either the author of the work or a person or organization that has obtained ownership of the copyright initially belonging to the author.

• ***Transfer:*** The statute provides that, if the copyright claimant is not the author, the application for registration must contain "a brief statement of how the claimant obtained ownership of the copyright." If any copyright claimant named in space 4 is not an author named in space 2, give a brief, general statement summarizing the means by which that claimant obtained ownership of the copyright.

FORM PA

UNITED STATES COPYRIGHT OFFICE

REGISTRATION NUMBER

PA PAU

EFFECTIVE DATE OF REGISTRATION

.... (Month) .... (Day) .... (Year)

DO NOT WRITE ABOVE THIS LINE. IF YOU NEED MORE SPACE, USE CONTINUATION SHEET (FORM PA/CON)

1 Title

TITLE OF THIS WORK: DANCE UNTIL IT HURTS

NATURE OF THIS WORK: (See instructions) Words and Music

PREVIOUS OR ALTERNATIVE TITLES: N/A

2 Author(s)

IMPORTANT: Under the law, the "author" of a "work made for hire" is generally the employer, not the employee (see instructions). If any part of this work was "made for hire" check "Yes" in the space provided, give the employer (or other person for whom the work was prepared) as "Author" of that part, and leave the space for dates blank.

1

NAME OF AUTHOR: John Gifted

Was this author's contribution to the work a "work made for hire"? Yes...... No X...

DATES OF BIRTH AND DEATH: Born 1953 (Year) Died .... (Year)

AUTHOR'S NATIONALITY OR DOMICILE: Citizen of U.S.A. (Name of Country) or Domiciled in .... (Name of Country)

WAS THIS AUTHOR'S CONTRIBUTION TO THE WORK: Anonymous? Yes...... No X... Pseudonymous? Yes...... No X...

AUTHOR OF: (Briefly describe nature of this author's contribution) Words and Music

If the answer to either of these questions is "Yes," see detailed instructions attached.

2

NAME OF AUTHOR:

Was this author's contribution to the work a "work made for hire"? Yes...... No......

DATES OF BIRTH AND DEATH: Born .... (Year) Died .... (Year)

AUTHOR'S NATIONALITY OR DOMICILE: Citizen of .... (Name of Country) or Domiciled in .... (Name of Country)

WAS THIS AUTHOR'S CONTRIBUTION TO THE WORK: Anonymous? Yes...... No...... Pseudonymous? Yes...... No......

AUTHOR OF: (Briefly describe nature of this author's contribution)

If the answer to either of these questions is "Yes," see detailed instructions attached.

3

NAME OF AUTHOR:

Was this author's contribution to the work a "work made for hire"? Yes...... No......

DATES OF BIRTH AND DEATH: Born .... (Year) Died .... (Year)

AUTHOR'S NATIONALITY OR DOMICILE: Citizen of .... (Name of Country) or Domiciled in .... (Name of Country)

WAS THIS AUTHOR'S CONTRIBUTION TO THE WORK: Anonymous? Yes...... No...... Pseudonymous? Yes...... No......

AUTHOR OF: (Briefly describe nature of this author's contribution)

If the answer to either of these questions is "Yes," see detailed instructions attached.

3 Creation and Publication

YEAR IN WHICH CREATION OF THIS WORK WAS COMPLETED: Year 1983

(This information must be given in all cases.)

DATE AND NATION OF FIRST PUBLICATION: Date N/A (Month) (Day) (Year)

Nation .... (Name of Country)

(Complete this block ONLY if this work has been published.)

4 Claimant(s)

NAME(S) AND ADDRESS(ES) OF COPYRIGHT CLAIMANT(S):

John Gifted
One Runningmill Lane
Topanga, CA 90000

TRANSFER: (If the copyright claimant(s) named here in space 4 are different from the author(s) named in space 2, give a brief statement of how the claimant(s) obtained ownership of the copyright.)

N/A

- *Complete all applicable spaces (numbers 5-9) on the reverse side of this page*
- *Follow detailed instructions attached*
- *Sign the form at line 8*

DO NOT WRITE HERE

Page 1 of .... pages

	EXAMINED BY: .... CHECKED BY:	APPLICATION RECEIVED:	FOR COPYRIGHT OFFICE USE ONLY
	CORRESPONDENCE: ☐ Yes	DEPOSIT RECEIVED:	
	DEPOSIT ACCOUNT FUNDS USED: ☐	REMITTANCE NUMBER AND DATE:	

DO NOT WRITE ABOVE THIS LINE. IF YOU NEED ADDITIONAL SPACE, USE CONTINUATION SHEET (FORM PA/CON)

5 Previous Registration

PREVIOUS REGISTRATION:

- Has registration for this work, or for an earlier version of this work, already been made in the Copyright Office? Yes .... No . X ......
- If your answer is "Yes," why is another registration being sought? (Check appropriate box)
  - ☐ This is the first published edition of a work previously registered in unpublished form.
  - ☐ This is the first application submitted by this author as copyright claimant.
  - ☐ This is a changed version of the work, as shown by line 6 of the application.
- If your answer is "Yes," give: Previous Registration Number .... Year of Registration ....

6 Compilation or Derivative Work

COMPILATION OR DERIVATIVE WORK: (See instructions)

PREEXISTING MATERIAL: (Identify any preexisting work or works that the work is based on or incorporates.)

N/A

MATERIAL ADDED TO THIS WORK: (Give a brief, general statement of the material that has been added to this work and in which copyright is claimed.)

N/A

7 Fee and Correspondence

DEPOSIT ACCOUNT: (If the registration fee is to be charged to a Deposit Account established in the Copyright Office, give name and number of Account.)

N/A

Name: ....

Account Number: ....

CORRESPONDENCE: (Give name and address to which correspondence about this application should be sent.)

Name: John Gifted

Address: One Runningmill Lane (Apt.)

Topanga, (City) CA (State) 90000 (ZIP)

8 Certification (Application must be signed)

CERTIFICATION: ✱ I, the undersigned, hereby certify that I am the: (Check one)

☒ author ☐ other copyright claimant ☐ owner of exclusive right(s) ☐ authorized agent of .... (Name of author or other copyright claimant, or owner of exclusive right(s))

of the work identified in this application and that the statements made by me in this application are correct to the best of my knowledge.

Handwritten signature: (X) John Gifted

Typed or printed name . John Gifted .... Date . 4/30/83

9 Address For Return of Certificate

John Gifted
(Name)
One Runningmill Lane
(Number, Street and Apartment Number)
Topanga, (City) CA (State) 90000 (ZIP code)

MAIL CERTIFICATE TO

(Certificate will be mailed in window envelope)

• 17 U.S.C. §506(e) FALSE REPRESENTATION—Any person who knowingly makes a false representation of a material fact in the application for copyright registration provided for by section 409, or in any written statement filed in connection with the application, shall be fined not more than $2,500

☆U.S. GOVERNMENT PRINTING OFFICE: 1980-311-425/2

Jan. 1980—500,000

CONTINUATION SHEET FOR FORM PA

FORM PA/CON

UNITED STATES COPYRIGHT OFFICE

- If at all possible, try to fit the information called for into the spaces provided on Form PA.
- If you do not have space enough for all of the information you need to give on Form PA, use this continuation sheet and submit it with Form PA.
- If you submit this continuation sheet, leave it attached to Form PA. Or, if it becomes detached, clip (do not tape or staple) and fold the two together before submitting them.
- **PART A** of this sheet is intended to identify the basic application. **PART B** is a continuation of Space 2. **PART C** is for the continuation of Spaces 1, 4, or 6. The other spaces on Form PA call for specific items of information, and should not need continuation.

REGISTRATION NUMBER	
PA	PAU
EFFECTIVE DATE OF REGISTRATION	
(Month) (Day) (Year)	
CONTINUATION SHEET RECEIVED	
Page ____ of ____ pages	

DO NOT WRITE ABOVE THIS LINE. FOR COPYRIGHT OFFICE USE ONLY

(A) Identification of Application

IDENTIFICATION OF CONTINUATION SHEET: This sheet is a continuation of the application for copyright registration on Form PA, submitted for the following work:

- TITLE: (Give the title as given under the heading "Title of this Work" in Space 1 of Form PA.)

....

- NAME(S) AND ADDRESS(ES) OF COPYRIGHT CLAIMANT(S): (Give the name and address of at least one copyright claimant as given in Space 4 of Form PA.)

....

(B) Continuation of Space 2

☐ **NAME OF AUTHOR:**

Was this author's contribution to the work a "work made for hire"? Yes...... No......

DATES OF BIRTH AND DEATH: Born .... (Year) Died .... (Year)

AUTHOR'S NATIONALITY OR DOMICILE: Citizen of .... (Name of Country) or Domiciled in .... (Name of Country)

WAS THIS AUTHOR'S CONTRIBUTION TO THE WORK: Anonymous? Yes...... No...... Pseudonymous? Yes...... No......

If the answer to either of these questions is "Yes," see detailed instructions attached.

AUTHOR OF: (Briefly describe nature of this author's contribution)

☐ **NAME OF AUTHOR:**

Was this author's contribution to the work a "work made for hire"? Yes...... No......

DATES OF BIRTH AND DEATH: Born .... (Year) Died .... (Year)

AUTHOR'S NATIONALITY OR DOMICILE: Citizen of .... (Name of Country) or Domiciled in .... (Name of Country)

WAS THIS AUTHOR'S CONTRIBUTION TO THE WORK: Anonymous? Yes...... No...... Pseudonymous? Yes...... No......

If the answer to either of these questions is "Yes," see detailed instructions attached.

AUTHOR OF: (Briefly describe nature of this author's contribution)

☐ **NAME OF AUTHOR:**

Was this author's contribution to the work a "work made for hire"? Yes...... No......

DATES OF BIRTH AND DEATH: Born .... (Year) Died .... (Year)

AUTHOR'S NATIONALITY OR DOMICILE: Citizen of .... (Name of Country) or Domiciled in .... (Name of Country)

WAS THIS AUTHOR'S CONTRIBUTION TO THE WORK: Anonymous? Yes...... No...... Pseudonymous? Yes...... No......

If the answer to either of these questions is "Yes," see detailed instructions attached.

AUTHOR OF: (Briefly describe nature of this author's contribution)

(C) Continuation of Other Spaces

CONTINUATION OF (Check which): ☐ Space 1 ☐ Space 4 ☐ Space 6

PRIVACY ACT ADVISORY STATEMENT
Required by the Privacy Act of 1974 (Public Law 93-579)

AUTHORITY FOR REQUESTING THIS INFORMATION:
- Title 17, U.S.C., Secs. 409 and 410

FURNISHING THE REQUESTED INFORMATION IS:
- Voluntary

BUT IF THE INFORMATION IS NOT FURNISHED:
- It may be necessary to delay or refuse registration
- You may not be entitled to certain relief, remedies, and benefits provided in chapters 4 and 5 of title 17, U.S.C.

PRINCIPAL USES OF REQUESTED INFORMATION:
- Establishment and maintenance of a public record
- Examination of the application for compliance with legal requirements

OTHER ROUTINE USES:
- Public inspection and copying
- Preparation of public indexes
- Preparation of public catalogs of copyright registrations
- Preparation of search reports upon request

NOTE:
- No other advisory statement will be given you in connection with this application
- Please retain this statement and refer to it if we communicate with you regarding this application

INSTRUCTIONS FOR SPACES 5-9

SPACE 5: PREVIOUS REGISTRATION

• ***General Instructions:*** The questions in space 5 are intended to find out whether an earlier registration has been made for this work and, if so, whether there is any basis for a new registration. As a general rule, only one basic copyright registration can be made for the same version of a particular work.

• ***Same Version:*** If this version is substantially the same as the work covered by a previous registration, a second registration is not generally possible unless: (1) the work has been registered in unpublished form and a second registration is now being sought to cover the first published edition, or (2) someone other than the author is identified as copyright claimant in the earlier registration, and the author is now seeking registration in his or her own name. If either of these two exceptions apply, check the appropriate box and give the earlier registration number and date. Otherwise, do not submit Form PA; instead, write the Copyright Office for information about supplementary registration or recordation of transfers of copyright ownership.

• ***Changed Version:*** If the work has been changed, and you are now seeking registration to cover the additions or revisions, check the third box in space 5, give the earlier registration number and date, and complete both parts of space 6.

• ***Previous Registration Number and Date:*** If more than one previous registration has been made for the work, give the number and date of the latest registration.

SPACE 6: COMPILATION OR DERIVATIVE WORK

• ***General Instructions:*** Complete both parts of space 6 if this work is a "compilation," or "derivative work," or both, and if it incorporates one or more earlier works that have already been published or registered for copyright, or that have fallen into the public domain. A "compilation" is defined as "a work formed by the collection and assembling of preexisting materials or of data that are selected, coordinated, or arranged in such a way that the resulting work as a whole constitutes an original work of authorship." A "derivative work" is "a work based on one or more preexisting works." Examples of derivative works include musical arrangements, dramatizations, translations, abridgments, condensations, motion picture versions, or "any other form in which a work may be recast, transformed, or adapted." Derivative works also include works "consisting of editorial revisions, annotations, elaborations, or other modifications" if these changes, as a whole, represent an original work of authorship.

• ***Preexisting Material:*** If the work is a compilation, give a brief, general statement describing the nature of the material that has been compiled. Example: "Compilation of 19th Century military songs." In the case of a derivative work, identify the preexisting work that has been recast, transformed, or adapted. Example: "French version of Hugo's 'Le Roi s'amuse'."

• ***Material Added to this Work:*** The statute requires a "brief, general statement of the additional material covered by the copyright claim being registered." This statement should describe all of the material in this particular version of the work that: (1) represents an original work of authorship; and (2) has not fallen into the public domain; and (3) has not been previously published; and (4) has not been previously registered for copyright in unpublished form. Examples: "Arrangement for piano and orchestra"; "Dramatization for television"; "New film version"; "Revisions throughout; Act III completely new".

SPACES 7, 8, 9: FEE, CORRESPONDENCE, CERTIFICATION, RETURN ADDRESS

• ***Deposit Account and Mailing Instructions (Space 7):*** If you maintain a Deposit Account in the Copyright Office, identify it in space 7. Otherwise you will need to send the registration fee of $10 with your application. The space headed "Correspondence" should contain the name and address of the person to be consulted if correspondence about this application becomes necessary.

• ***Certification (Space 8):*** The application is not acceptable unless it bears the handwritten signature of the author or other copyright claimant, or of the owner of exclusive right(s), or of the duly authorized agent of such author, claimant, or owner.

• ***Address for Return of Certificate (Space 9):*** The address box must be completed legibly, since the certificate will be returned in a window envelope.

MORE INFORMATION

A NOTE ON TERMINOLOGY: The following are the meanings given to some o the terms used in the copyright statute:

• ***"Works":*** "Works" are the basic subject matter of copyright; they are wha authors create and copyright protects. The statute draws a sharp distinction be tween the "work" and "any material object in which the work is embodied."

• ***"Copies" and "Phonorecords":*** These are the two types of material ob jects in which "works" are embodied. In general, **"copies"** are objects from which a work can be read or visually perceived, directly or with the aid of a machine or device, such as manuscripts, books, sheet music, film, and video tape. **"Phonorecords"** are objects embodying fixations of sounds, such as au dio tapes and phonograph disks. For example, a song (the "work") can be repro duced in sheet music ("copies") or phonograph disks ("phonorecords"), or both.

• ***"Sound Recordings":*** These are "works," not "copies" or "phonorecords." With one exception, "sound recordings" are "works that result from the fixation o a series of musical, spoken, or other sounds." (The exception is for the audio por tions of audiovisual works, including motion picture soundtracks; these are con sidered an integral part of the audiovisual work as a whole.) "Sound recordings" are registered on Form SR.

Example: When a record company issues a new release, the release will typi cally involve two distinct "works": the "musical work" that has been recorded, and the "sound recording" as a separate work in itself. The material objects that the record company sends out are "phonorecords": physical reproductions of both the "musical work" and the "sound recording."

FOR A MUSICAL OR DRAMATIC WORK, SHOULD YOU DEPOSIT COPIES OR PHONORECORDS WITH YOUR FORM PA?

• ***For registration in unpublished form:***

(1) If the work exists only in one form or the other (copies or phonorecords but not both), deposit the work in its existing form;

(2) If the work exists in both copies and phonorecords, deposit the form that best represents the musical or dramatic work in which copyright is being claimed.

• ***For registration in published form:***

(1) If the work has been published in the form of copies but not phono records, deposit two copies of the best edition. If the work has been published in the form of phonorecords only, deposit two phonorecords of the best edition.

(2) If the work has been published in both forms, deposit two copies (**not phonorecords**) of the best edition.

(3) If the work has been first published outside the United States, deposit one copy or phonorecord as first published.

SHOULD YOU FILE FORM PA OR FORM SR? If the musical or dramatic work has been recorded, and both that "work," and the sound recording as a sep arate "work," are eligible for registration, the application form you should file de pends on the following:

• ***File only Form PA if:*** You are seeking to register only the musical or dra matic work, not the sound recording.

• ***File only Form SR if:*** The copyright claimant for both the musical or dra matic work and the sound recording is the same, and you are seeking a single regis tration to cover both of these "works."

• ***Separate applications on Forms PA and SR should be filed if:***

(1) The copyright claimant for the musical or dramatic work is different from the copyright claimant for the sound recording; or

(2) You prefer to have separate registrations for the musical or dramatic work **and** the sound recording.

FORM OF COPYRIGHT NOTICE ON PHONORECORDS:

For musical or dramatic works: The copyright notice for musical and dra matic works (for example: "© 1978 George Harvey Bone") is required to appear on "all publicly distributed copies from which the work can be visually perceived." There is no requirement that the notice for musical or dramatic works be placed on phonorecords reproducing them.

For sound recordings: The copyright statute provides that, whenever a sound recording is published, a special notice of copyright (for example "℗1978 Miriam Haines") "shall be placed on all publicly distributed phonorecords of the sound recording." For further information about the requirements for copyright in sound recordings, write for Form SR.

Filling Out Application Form SR

Detach and read these instructions before completing this form. Make sure all applicable spaces have been filled in before you return this form.

BASIC INFORMATION

When to Use This Form: Use Form SR for copyright registration of published or unpublished sound recordings. It should be used where the copyright claim is limited to the sound recording itself, and it may also be used where the same copyright claimant is seeking simultaneous registration of the underlying musical, dramatic, or literary work embodied in the phonorecord.

With one exception, "sound recordings" are works that result from the fixation of a series of musical, spoken, or other sounds. The exception is for the audio portions of audiovisual works, such as a motion picture soundtrack or an audio cassette accompanying a filmstrip; these are considered a part of the audiovisual work as a whole.

Deposit to Accompany Application: An application for copyright registration of a sound recording must be accompanied by a deposit consisting of phonorecords representing the entire work for which registration is to be made.

Unpublished Work: Deposit one complete phonorecord.

Published Work: Deposit two complete phonorecords of the best edition, together with "any printed or other visually perceptible material" published with the phonorecords.

Work First Published Outside the United States: Deposit one complete phonorecord of the first foreign edition.

Contribution to a Collective Work: Deposit one complete phonorecord of the best edition of the collective work.

The Copyright Notice: For published sound recordings, the law provides that a copyright notice in a specified form "shall be placed on all publicly distributed phonorecords of the sound recording." Use of the copyright notice is the responsibility of the copyright owner and does not require advance permission from the Copyright Office. The required form of the notice for phonorecords of sound recordings consists of three elements: (1) the symbol "℗" (the letter "P" in a circle); (2) the year of first publication of the sound recording; and (3) the name of the owner of copyright. For example: "℗ 1981 Rittenhouse Record Co." The notice is to be "placed on the surface of the phonorecord, or on the label or container, in such manner and location as to give reasonable notice of the claim of copyright." For further information about copyright, write:
Information and Publications Section, LM-455
Copyright Office, Library of Congress, Washington, D.C. 20559

PRIVACY ACT ADVISORY STATEMENT Required by the Privacy Act of 1974 (P.L. 93-579)

The authority for requesting this information is title 17, U.S.C., secs. 409 and 410. Furnishing the requested information is voluntary. But if the information is not furnished, it may be necessary to delay or refuse registration and you may not be entitled to certain relief, remedies, and benefits provided in chapters 4 and 5 of title 17, U.S.C.

The principal uses of the requested information are the establishment and maintenance of a public record and the examination of the application for compliance with legal requirements.

Other routine uses include public inspection and copying, preparation of public indexes, preparation of public catalogs of copyright registrations, and preparation of search reports upon request.

NOTE: No other advisory statement will be given in connection with this application. Please keep this statement and refer to it if we communicate with you regarding this application.

LINE-BY-LINE INSTRUCTIONS

1 SPACE 1: Title

Title of This Work: Every work submitted for copyright registration must be given a title to identify that particular work. If the phonorecords or any accompanying printed material bear a title (or an identifying phrase that could serve as a title), transcribe that wording completely and exactly on the application. Indexing of the registration and future identification of the work may depend on the information you give here.

Nature of Material Recorded: Indicate the general type or character of the works or other material embodied in the recording. The box marked "Literary" should be checked for nondramatic spoken material of all sorts, including narration, interviews, panel discussions, and training material. If the material recorded is not musical, dramatic, or literary in nature, check "Other" and briefly describe the type of sounds fixed in the recording. For example: "Sound Effects"; "Bird Calls"; "Crowd Noises."

Previous or Alternative Titles: Complete this space if there are any additional titles for the work under which someone searching for the registration might be likely to look, or under which a document pertaining to the work might be recorded.

2 SPACE 2: Author(s)

General Instructions: After reading these instructions, decide who are the "authors" of this work for copyright purposes. Then, unless the work is a "collective work," give the requested information about every "author" who contributed any appreciable amount of copyrightable matter to this version of the work. If you need further space, request additional Continuation Sheets. In the case of a collective work, such as a collection of previously published or registered sound recordings, give information about the author of the collective work as a whole. If you are submitting this Form SR to cover the recorded musical, dramatic, or literary work as well as the sound recording itself, it is important for space 2 to include full information about the various authors of all of the material covered by the copyright claim, making clear the nature of each author's contribution.

Name of Author: The fullest form of the author's name should be given. Unless the work was "made for hire," the individual who actually created the work is its "author." In the case of a work made for hire, the statute provides that "the employer or other person for whom the work was prepared is considered the author."

What is a "Work Made for Hire"? A "work made for hire" is defined as: (1) "a work prepared by an employee within the scope of his or her employment"; or (2) "a work specially ordered or commissioned for use as a contribution to a collective work, as a part of a motion picture or other audiovisual work, as a translation, as a supplementary work, as a compilation, as an instructional text, as a test, as answer material for a test, or as an atlas, if the parties expressly agree in a written instrument signed by them that the work shall be considered a work made for hire." If you have checked "Yes" to indicate that the work was "made for hire," you must give the full legal name of the employer (or other person for whom the work was prepared). You may also include the name of the employee along with the name of the employer (for example: "Elster Record Co., employer for hire of John Ferguson").

"Anonymous" or "Pseudonymous" Work: An author's contribution to a work is "anonymous" if that author is not identified on the copies or phonorecords of the work. An author's contribution to a work is "pseudonymous" if that author is identified on the copies or phonorecords under a fictitious name. If the work is "anonymous" you may: (1) leave the line blank; or (2) state "anonymous" on the line; or (3) reveal the author's identity. If the work is "pseudonymous" you may: (1) leave the line blank; or (2) give the pseudonym and identify it as such (for example: "Huntley Haverstock, pseudonym"); or (3) reveal the author's name, making clear which is the real name and which is the pseudonym (for example: "Judith Barton, whose pseudonym is Madeline Elster"). However, the citizenship or domicile of the author **must** be given in all cases.

Dates of Birth and Death: If the author is dead, the statute requires that the year of death be included in the application unless the work is anonymous or pseudonymous. The author's birth date is optional, but is useful as a form of identification. Leave this space blank if the author's contribution was a "work made for hire."

Author's Nationality or Domicile: Give the country of which the author is a citizen, or the country in which the author is domiciled. Nationality or domicile **must** be given in all cases.

Nature of Authorship: Give a brief general statement of the nature of this particular author's contribution to the work. If you are submitting this Form SR to cover both the sound recording and the underlying musical, dramatic, or literary work, make sure that the precise nature of each author's contribution is reflected here. Examples where the authorship pertains to the recording: "Sound Recording"; "Performance and Recording"; "Compilation and Remixing of Sounds." Examples where the authorship pertains to both the recording and the underlying work: "Words, Music, Performance, Recording"; "Arrangement of Music and Recording"; "Compilation of Poems and Reading."

3 SPACE 3: Creation and Publication

General Instructions: Do not confuse "creation" with "publication." Every application for copyright registration must state "the year in which creation of the work was completed." Give the date and nation of first publication only if the work has been published.

Creation: Under the statute, a work is "created" when it is fixed in a copy or phonorecord for the first time. Where a work has been prepared over a period of time, the part of the work existing in fixed form on a particular date constitutes the created work on that date. The date you give here should be the year in which the author completed the particular version for which registration is now being sought, even if other versions exist or if further changes or additions are planned.

Publication: The statute defines "publication" as "the distribution of copies or phonorecords of a work to the public by sale or other transfer of ownership, or by rental, lease, or lending"; a work is also "published" if there has been an "offering to distribute copies or phonorecords to a group of persons for purposes of further distribution, public performance, or public display." Give the full date (month, day, year) when, and the country where, publication first occurred. If first publication took place simultaneously in the United States and other countries, it is sufficient to state "U.S.A."

4 SPACE 4: Claimant(s)

Name(s) and Address(es) of Copyright Claimant(s): Give the name(s) and address(es) of the copyright claimant(s) in this work even if the claimant is the same as the author. Copyright in a work belongs initially to the author of the work (including, in the case of a work made for hire, the employer or other person for whom the work was prepared). The copyright claimant is either the author of the work or a person or organization to whom the copyright initially belonging to the author has been transferred.

Transfer: The statute provides that, if the copyright claimant is not the author, the application for registration must contain "a brief statement of how the claimant obtained ownership of the copyright." If any copyright claimant named in space 4 is not an author named in space 2, give a brief, general statement summarizing the means by which that claimant obtained ownership of the copyright. Examples: "By written contract"; "Transfer of all rights by author"; "Assignment"; "By will." Do not attach transfer documents or other attachments or riders.

5 SPACE 5: Previous Registration

General Instructions: The questions in space 5 are intended to find out whether an earlier registration has been made for this work and, if so, whether there is any basis for a new registration. As a rule, only one basic copyright registration can be made for the same version of a particular work.

Same Version: If this version is substantially the same as the work covered by a previous registration, a second registration is not generally possible unless: (1) the work has been registered in unpublished form and a second registration is now being sought to cover this first published edition; or (2) someone other than the author is identified as copyright claimant in the earlier registration, and the author is now seeking registration in his or her own name. If either of these two exceptions apply, check the appropriate box and give the earlier registration number and date. Otherwise, do not submit Form SR; instead, write the Copyright Office for information about supplementary registration or recordation of transfers of copyright ownership.

Changed Version: If the work has been changed, and you are now seeking registration to cover the additions or revisions, check the last box in space 5, give the earlier registration number and date, and complete both parts of space 6 in accordance with the instructions below.

Previous Registration Number and Date: If more than one previous registration has been made for the work, give the number and date of the latest registration.

6 SPACE 6: Derivative Work or Compilation

General Instructions: Complete space 6 if this work is a "changed version," "compilation," or "derivative work," and if it incorporates one or more earlier works that have already been published or registered for copyright, or that have fallen into the public domain, or sound recordings that were fixed before February 15, 1972. A "compilation" is defined as "a work formed by the collection and assembling of preexisting materials or of data that are selected, coordinated, or arranged in such a way that the resulting work as a whole constitutes an original work of authorship." A "derivative work" is "a work based on one or more preexisting works." Examples of derivative works include recordings reissued with substantial editorial revisions or abridgments of the recorded sounds, and recordings republished with new recorded material, or "any other form in which a work may be recast, transformed, or adapted." Derivative works also include works "consisting of editorial revisions, annotations, or other modifications" if these changes, as a whole, represent an original work of authorship.

Preexisting Material (space 6a): Complete this space **and** space 6b for derivative works. In this space identify the preexisting work that has been recast, transformed, or adapted. For example, the preexisting material might be: "1970 recording by Sperryville Symphony of Bach Double Concerto." Do not complete this space for compilations.

Material Added to This Work (space 6b): Give a brief, general statement of the **additional** new material covered by the copyright claim for which registration is sought. In the case of a derivative work, identify this new material. Examples: "Recorded performances on bands 1 and 3"; "Remixed sounds from original multitrack sound sources"; "New words, arrangement, and additional sounds." If the work is a compilation, give a brief, general statement describing both the material that has been compiled **and** the compilation itself. Example: "Compilation of 1938 Recordings by various swing bands."

7,8,9 SPACE 7, 8, 9: Fee, Correspondence, Certification, Return Address

Deposit Account: If you maintain a Deposit Account in the Copyright Office, identify it in space 7. Otherwise leave the space blank and send the fee of $10 with your application and deposit.

Correspondence (space 7): This space should contain the name, address, area code, and telephone number of the person to be consulted if correspondence about this application becomes necessary.

Certification (space 8): The application cannot be accepted unless it bears the date and the **handwritten signature** of the author or other copyright claimant, or of the owner of exclusive right(s), or of the duly authorized agent of the author, claimant, or owner of exclusive right(s).

Address for Return of Certificate (space 9): The address box must be completed legibly since the certificate will be returned in a window envelope.

MORE INFORMATION

"Works": "Works" are the basic subject matter of copyright; they are what authors create and copyright protects. The statute draws a sharp distinction between the "work" and "any material object in which the work is embodied."

"Copies" and "Phonorecords": These are the two types of material objects in which "works" are embodied. In general, **"copies"** are objects from which a work can be read or visually perceived, directly or with the aid of a machine or device, such as manuscripts, books, sheet music, film, and videotape. **"Phonorecords"** are objects embodying fixations of sounds, such as audio tapes and phonograph disks. For example, a song (the "work") can be reproduced in sheet music ("copies") or phonograph disks ("phonorecords"), or both.

"Sound Recordings": These are "works," not "copies" or "phonorecords." "Sound recordings" are "works that result from the fixation of a series of musical, spoken, or other sounds, but not including the sounds accompanying a motion picture or other audiovisual work." Example: When a record company issues a new release, the release will typically involve two distinct "works": the "musical work" that has been recorded, and the "sound recording" as a separate work in itself. The material objects that the record company sends out are "phonorecords": physical reproductions of both the "musical work" and the "sound recording."

Should You File More Than One Application?

If your work consists of a recorded musical, dramatic, or literary work, and both that "work," and the sound recording as a separate "work," are eligible for registration, the application form you should file depends on the following:

File Only Form SR if: The copyright claimant is the same for both the musical, dramatic, or literary work and for the sound recording, and you are seeking a single registration to cover both of these "works."

File Only Form PA (or Form TX) if: You are seeking to register only the musical, dramatic, or literary work, not the sound recording. Form PA is appropriate for works of the performing arts; Form TX is for nondramatic literary works.

Separate Applications Should Be Filed on Form PA (or Form TX) and on Form SR if: (1) The copyright claimant for the musical, dramatic, or literary work is different from the copyright claimant for the sound recording; or (2) You prefer to have separate registrations for the musical, dramatic, or literary work and for the sound recording.

FORM SR
UNITED STATES COPYRIGHT OFFICE

REGISTRATION NUMBER

SR SRU

EFFECTIVE DATE OF REGISTRATION

Month Day Year

DO NOT WRITE ABOVE THIS LINE. IF YOU NEED MORE SPACE, USE A SEPARATE CONTINUATION SHEET.

1

TITLE OF THIS WORK ▼

DANCE UNTIL IT HURTS

PREVIOUS OR ALTERNATIVE TITLES ▼

N/A

NATURE OF MATERIAL RECORDED ▼ See instructions.

☒ Musical ☐ Musical-Dramatic
☐ Dramatic ☐ Literary
☐ Other ________

2

a **NAME OF AUTHOR ▼** John Gifted

DATES OF BIRTH AND DEATH Year Born ▼ 1953 Year Died ▼

Was this contribution to the work a "work made for hire"? ☐ Yes ☒ No

AUTHOR'S NATIONALITY OR DOMICILE Name of Country
OR { Citizen of ▶ U.S.A. / Domiciled in ▶ ________

WAS THIS AUTHOR'S CONTRIBUTION TO THE WORK
Anonymous? ☐ Yes ☒ No
Pseudonymous? ☐ Yes ☒ No
If the answer to either of these questions is "Yes," see detailed instructions.

NATURE OF AUTHORSHIP Briefly describe nature of the material created by this author in which copyright is claimed. ▼
Words, Music, Performance, Recording

NOTE
Under the law, the "author" of a "work made for hire" is generally the employer, not the employee (see instructions). For any part of this work that was "made for hire" check "Yes" in the space provided, give the employer (or other person for whom the work was prepared) as "Author" of that part, and leave the space for dates of birth and death blank.

b **NAME OF AUTHOR ▼**

DATES OF BIRTH AND DEATH Year Born ▼ Year Died ▼

Was this contribution to the work a "work made for hire"? ☐ Yes ☒ No

AUTHOR'S NATIONALITY OR DOMICILE Name of country
OR { Citizen of ▶ ________ / Domiciled in ▶ ________

WAS THIS AUTHOR'S CONTRIBUTION TO THE WORK
Anonymous? ☐ Yes ☐ No
Pseudonymous? ☐ Yes ☐ No
If the answer to either of these questions is "Yes," see detailed instructions.

NATURE OF AUTHORSHIP Briefly describe nature of the material created by this author in which copyright is claimed. ▼

c **NAME OF AUTHOR ▼**

DATES OF BIRTH AND DEATH Year Born ▼ Year Died ▼

Was this contribution to the work a "work made for hire"? ☐ Yes ☐ No

AUTHOR'S NATIONALITY OR DOMICILE Name of Country
OR { Citizen of ▶ ________ / Domiciled in ▶ ________

WAS THIS AUTHOR'S CONTRIBUTION TO THE WORK
Anonymous? ☐ Yes ☐ No
Pseudonymous? ☐ Yes ☐ No
If the answer to either of these questions is "Yes," see detailed instructions.

NATURE OF AUTHORSHIP Briefly describe nature of the material created by this author in which copyright is claimed. ▼

3

YEAR IN WHICH CREATION OF THIS WORK WAS COMPLETED **This information must be given in all cases.**
1983 ◀ Year

DATE AND NATION OF FIRST PUBLICATION OF THIS PARTICULAR WORK
Complete this information ONLY if this work has been published. Month ▶ N/A Day ▶ ____ Year ▶ ____
________ ◀ Nation

4

COPYRIGHT CLAIMANT(S) Name and address must be given even if the claimant is the same as the author given in space 2.▼

John Gifted
One Runningmill Lane
Topanga, CA 90000

See instructions before completing this space.

TRANSFER If the claimant(s) named here in space 4 are different from the author(s) named in space 2, give a brief statement of how the claimant(s) obtained ownership of the copyright.▼

N/A

DO NOT WRITE HERE OFFICE USE ONLY

APPLICATION RECEIVED

ONE DEPOSIT RECEIVED

TWO DEPOSITS RECEIVED

REMITTANCE NUMBER AND DATE

MORE ON BACK ▶
• Complete all applicable spaces (numbers 5-9) on the reverse side of this page.
• See detailed instructions. • Sign the form at line 8.

DO NOT WRITE HERE

Page 1 of ________ pages

EXAMINED BY

CHECKED BY

☐ CORRESPONDENCE Yes

☐ DEPOSIT ACCOUNT FUNDS USED

FORM SR

FOR COPYRIGHT OFFICE USE ONLY

DO NOT WRITE ABOVE THIS LINE. IF YOU NEED MORE SPACE, USE A SEPARATE CONTINUATION SHEET.

5

PREVIOUS REGISTRATION Has registration for this work, or for an earlier version of this work, already been made in the Copyright Office?

☐ **Yes** ☒ **No** If your answer is "Yes," why is another registration being sought? (Check appropriate box) ▼

☐ This is the first published edition of a work previously registered in unpublished form.

☐ This is the first application submitted by this author as copyright claimant.

☐ This is a changed version of the work, as shown by space 6 on this application.

If your answer is "Yes," give: **Previous Registration Number** ▼ **Year of Registration** ▼

6

DERIVATIVE WORK OR COMPILATION Complete both space 6a & 6b for a derivative work; complete only 6b for a compilation.

a. **Preexisting Material** Identify any preexisting work or works that this work is based on or incorporates. ▼

N/A

See instructions before completing this space.

b. **Material Added to This Work** Give a brief, general statement of the material that has been added to this work and in which copyright is claimed. ▼

N/A

7

DEPOSIT ACCOUNT If the registration fee is to be charged to a Deposit Account established in the Copyright Office, give name and number of Account.

Name ▼ N/A **Account Number** ▼

CORRESPONDENCE Give name and address to which correspondence about this application should be sent. Name/Address/Apt/City/State/Zip ▼

John Gifted
One Runningmill Lane
Topanga, CA 90000

Area Code & Telephone Number ▶ (111)555-7438

Be sure to give your daytime phone ◀ number.

8

CERTIFICATION* I, the undersigned, hereby certify that I am the

Check one ▼

☒ author

☐ other copyright claimant

☐ owner of exclusive right(s)

☐ authorized agent of ______________________
Name of author or other copyright claimant, or owner of exclusive right(s) ▲

of the work identified in this application and that the statements made by me in this application are correct to the best of my knowledge.

Typed or printed name and date ▼ If this is a published work, this date must be the same as or later than the date of publication given in space 3.

John Gifted **date** ▶ 4/30/83

Handwritten signature (X) ▼ John Gifted

9

MAIL CERTIFICATE TO

Name ▼
John Gifted

Number/Street/Apartment Number ▼
One Runningmill Lane

City/State/ZIP ▼
Topanga, CA 90000

Certificate will be mailed in window envelope

Have you:

- Completed all necessary spaces?
- Signed your application in space 8?
- Enclosed check or money order for $10 payable to *Register of Copyrights*?
- Enclosed your deposit material with the application and fee?

MAIL TO: Register of Copyrights, Library of Congress, Washington, D.C. 20559

* 17 U.S.C. § 506(e): Any person who knowingly makes a false representation of a material fact in the application for copyright registration provided for by section 409, or in any written statement filed in connection with the application, shall be fined not more than $2,500.

✩ U.S. GOVERNMENT PRINTING OFFICE: 1981-355-310

Circular R50

Copyright Registration for Musical Compositions

GENERAL INFORMATION

The copyright law of the United States (title 17 of the United States Code) provides for copyright in "musical works, including any accompanying words," which are fixed in some tangible medium of expression. Musical works include both original compositions and original arrangements or other new versions of earlier compositions to which new copyrightable authorship has been added.

How Copyright Is Secured

The Copyright Office registers claims to copyrights and issues certificates of registration, but does not "grant" or "issue" copyrights. Under the present statute, copyright protection begins at the time a work is created in a fixed form such as a writing or recording.

Original musical works may be registered in published or unpublished form. For unpublished works and works published on or after January 1, 1978, registration in the Copyright Office is not a condition of protection; however, there are certain advantages. This circular is designed to assist those who wish to register a claim to copyright in a musical composition.

Publication

The present Copyright Act defines publication as follows:

> "Publication is the distribution of copies or phonorecords of a work to the public by sale or other transfer of ownership, or by rental, lease, or lending. The offering to distribute copies or phonorecords to a group of persons for purposes of further distribution, public performance, or public display, constitutes publication. A public performance or display of a work does not of itself constitute publication."

"To the public" generally means to persons under no explicit or implicit restrictions with respect to disclosure. The following acts do *not* constitute publication: performance of the work, preparation of copies or phonorecords, or sending the work to the Copyright Office.

The above definition of publication applies *only* to works governed by the copyright law which took effect January 1, 1978. Prior to 1978, musical compositions were considered published when copies (not phonorecords) were sold, placed on sale, or publicly distributed under the authority of the copyright owner. Works first published before 1978 can be registered only if the published copies bore a copyright notice in the prescribed form and location.

Phonorecords were not considered "copies" of musical compositions under the law in effect through December 31, 1977. The sale or public distribution of phonorecords, therefore, did *not* publish the musical composition that was embodied in them. If, however, phonorecords distributed prior to 1978 were still being sold or were publicly available on January 1, 1978, the underlying musical composition was considered published as of January 1, 1978. For purposes of registration, the date of publication for a musical work embodied in such a phonorecord is January 1, 1978. Where phonorecords were no longer available on January 1, 1978, but were reissued later, the reissue date is the date of first publication.

REGISTRATION PROCEDURES

If you choose to register a claim in your work, send the following material in the same envelope or package to the Register of Copyrights, Copyright Office, Library of Congress, Washington, D.C. 20559:

1. A properly completed application form;
2. A non-returnable deposit of the work to be registered; and
3. A fee of $10 with each application.

Application Form

Form PA is the appropriate form for registration, whether it is accompanied by the deposit of a "copy" (lead sheet or sheet music) or a "phonorecord" (disk or tape). Only original Copyright Office forms will be accepted for registration; photocopied forms are not acceptable. The form should be completed with pen-and-ink (preferably black) or typewriter. Do not use pencil or send a carbon copy. All pertinent information should be supplied on the basic application form. A continuation sheet supplied by the Copyright Office should be used only when all necessary information cannot be recorded on the basic application form. No other attachments will be accepted.

Form SR is for registration of "sound recordings." A sound recording is a work that results from the fixation of a series of sounds. The author of a sound recording is the performer, or the record producer, or both. Form SR may be used to register both a musical work and a sound recording fixed in a phonorecord, provided that the same person or organization owns the copyrights in both works. If both kinds of work are being registered, space 2 of Form SR must clearly account for the authorship of both the musical composition (music, or words and music) *and* the sound recording (performance, sound recording, or both).

How To Complete Form PA

Instructions for completing each space of the application accompany the form. Nevertheless, registration is often delayed because of mistakes in filling out the form. The following points should be noted in particular:

Space 1: Give the title of the work exactly as it appears on the copy or phonorecord.

- A group of ***unpublished*** works registered as a collection must be given a collection title. The individual titles may be given on a Continuation Sheet.
- For registration of an entire collection of ***published*** works, give the title of the collection.
- For registration of only some of the individual works in a published collection, give the titles of the individual works, followed by "Contained in (title of collection)."

See the section in this circular under "Collections of Music" for further information.

Space 2: Answer carefully the question "was this author's contribution to the work a work made for hire?" Check "yes" ***only*** if that contribution was either (1) prepared by an employee within the scope of his or her employment or (2) specially ordered for a certain use, with an express written agreement signed by both parties that the work shall be considered a work made for hire. Such certain uses include contributions to a collective work, parts of a motion picture or other audiovisual work, or supplementary works such as new musical arrangements. If the contribution was made for hire, give the name of the ***employer***, not the person who actually did the writing, in the "Name of Author" box.

Complete the "Nature of Authorship" space to specify what the author created as written or recorded in the copy or phonorecord that accompanies the application. Examples are: "music," "words," "arrangement." Do ***not*** include elements not present in that copy or phonorecord. Do ***not*** include elements that are not protected by copyright such as an idea, concept, name, or title.

Space 3: *Creation*. The year of creation is the year in which the version of the work to be registered was ***first*** fixed in writing or recorded in any other tangible form. ***This year date must always be given***.

Publication. The definition of "publication" is discussed earlier in this circular (page 2). If publication has not taken place, ***leave this box blank***. If the version of the work being registered has been published, give the month, day, and year when copies or phonorecords were first published.

Space 4: The ***name*** and ***address*** of the ***copyright claimant must be given***. The copyright claimant is either the author or a person or organization to whom the author has transferred ***all*** of the rights in the United States copyright. When the claimant named is ***not*** the author, a brief transfer statement is required at space 4 to show how the claimant acquired the copyright. Examples of generally acceptable statements include: "by written agreement"; "assignment"; "written contract"; "by will." Do not attach copies of documents of transfer of copyright to the application. If you wish information on how to record transfers or other documents pertaining to a copyright, write to the Copyright Office for Circular R12.

When the name of the claimant is not the name of the author given at space 2, but the two names identify one person, the relationship between the names should be explained at space 4. Examples are: "Doe Publishing Company, solely owned by John Doe"; or "John Doe doing business as Doe Publishing Company."

Space 5: The first question should be answered "yes" ***only*** if a previous registration for the work being registered or another version of this work was completed and a certificate of copyright registration issued. If this is the case, check the appropriate box to show why another registration is sought; ***and*** give the requested information about the previous registration.

If no previous registration was completed, answer the first question "no" and leave the rest of space 5 blank.

Space 6: Complete this space only if the work being registered contains a ***substantial*** amount of material

(1) that was previously published; or

(2) that was previously registered in the United States Copyright Office; or

(3) that is in the public domain.

Leave this space blank if the work does not contain a substantial amount of any of these three kinds of material.

Space 6a: Complete this space and space 6b for derivative works. In space 6a briefly describe the preexisting material that has been recast, transformed, or adapted.

Space 6b: For derivative works, complete this space by stating briefly but clearly ***all*** of the added or revised copyrightable material which forms the basis of the present registration. Examples: "Arrangement for piano and orchestra" or "new lyric."

For compilations, give a brief, general statement describing both the material that has been compiled ***and*** the compilation itself. Example: "Compilation of selected 19th century military songs."

Space 2 must include information about the authorship of this new material.

Space 8: The application must bear an original signature and be dated. Stamped or printed signatures are not acceptable. For a published work, the application must be certified on or after the date of first publication. If the certification date is earlier than the date of publication given at space 3, the application cannot be accepted.

DEPOSIT REQUIREMENTS

The application must be accompanied by a deposit of the work to be registered. The deposit requirement varies according to the type of work for which registration is sought. Deposits cannot be returned.

Unpublished Works

Deposit one complete copy (lead sheet or sheet music) or phonorecord (disk or tape). "Complete" means including everything that is to be covered by the registration. A copyright registration generally covers only the material that is deposited for registration although the copyright law automatically gives copyright protection to all copyrightable authorship that is fixed in a copy or phonorecord. Copies should be legible, and both words and music on a phonorecord should be clear and audible. All deposits should bear the title of the work. Copies of a group of works registered as a collection should be assembled in orderly form and fastened together or placed in a folder. The title of a collection should appear on copies and phonorecords.

Published Works

If the work was first published in the United States on or after January 1, 1978, deposit two complete copies or phonorecords of the best edition. In the case of a work published by rental, lease, or lending, deposit one complete copy. Where rental is of a full score and parts, or a conductor's score and parts, the full score or conductor's score is a "complete" copy.

If the work is a contribution to a collective work, and published on or after January 1, 1978, deposit one complete copy or phonorecord of the best edition of the collective work.

If the work was first published in the United States before January 1, 1978, deposit two complete copies of the best edition of the work *as first published*.

If the work is a contribution to a collective work, and published prior to January 1, 1978, deposit one complete copy of the collective work as first published.

If the work was first published outside the United States, whenever published, deposit one complete copy or phonorecord of the work as first published.

For separate registration of a musical composition published *only* in a motion picture soundtrack, deposit: (1) a transcription of the entire work, or a reproduction of the entire work on a phonorecord; and (2) photographs or other reproductions from the motion picture of the title of the motion picture, the soundtrack credits, and the copyright notice for the soundtrack if any. Deposit of the entire motion picture is not required.

FEE

A fee prescribed by the copyright law is required for each work submitted to be registered for copyright. The fee, currently $10, is not refundable if the claim to copyright is refused registration under section 410(b) of the Copyright Act. A check or money order should be made payable to the Register of Copyrights. Do not send cash.

COLLECTIONS OF MUSIC

Unpublished Collections

To register two or more unpublished musical compositions with one application and fee, *all* of the following conditions *must* be met.

1. The selections must be assembled in an orderly form.
2. The combined selections must bear a single title identifying the collection as a whole.
3. The copyright claimant or claimants must be the same for each selection.
4. All of the selections must be by the same author, or, if they are by different authors, at least one author must have contributed to each selection.

Note that while the authorship may be different for different selections (provided that at least one author contributed to all of them), the ownership must be exactly the same for each selection. When a group of unpublished works is registered as a collection, only the collection title will appear in the catalogs and indexes of the Copyright Office. Individual titles will appear in Copyright Office records only if separate registrations are made for each work or if an application for supplementary registration is submitted to specify the individual titles in a collection. An application for supplementary registration may not be submitted until a certificate of registration has been issued for the collection. For more information on supplementary registration, please request Circular R8 and application Form CA.

Published Collections

A published collection of musical compositions may be registered with one application and fee if all of the compositions are owned by the same copyright claimant. The entire collection may be registered under the collection title.

NOTICE OF COPYRIGHT

When a musical work is published under the authority of the copyright owner, the copyright owner should make certain that a notice of copyright is placed on all publicly distributed copies. This notice is required even on works published outside of the United States. Failure to comply with the notice requirement can result in the loss of certain additional rights otherwise available to the copyright owner.

Affixing the copyright notice to copies to be published is the responsibility of the copyright owner and does not require advance permission from, or registration with, the Copyright Office.

Form of Notice for Visually Perceptible Copies

The copyright notice for visually perceptible copies should contain the following three elements:

1. The symbol "©" (the letter C in a circle), or the word "Copyright," or the abbreviation "Copr."; *and*

2. The year of first publication of the work (Note: In the case of compilations or derivative works incorporating previously published material, the year date of first publication of the compilation or derivative work is sufficient); *and*

3. The name of the owner of copyright in the work, or an abbreviation by which the name can be recognized, or a generally known alternative designation of the owner.

Example: © 1982 John Doe

The "C in a circle" notice is required only on "visually perceptible copies." There is no requirement that the phonorecord bear a "C in a circle" notice to protect the underlying musical, dramatic, or literary work that is recorded.

The notice should be affixed to copies of the work in such a manner and location as to "give reasonable notice of the claim of copyright." The three elements of the notice should ordinarily appear together on the copies. The Copyright Office has issued regulations concerning the form and position of the copyright notice in the *Code of Federal Regulations* (37 C.F.R. Part 201); for copies of these regulations, write to the Information and Publications Section, LM-455, Copyright Office, Library of Congress, Washington, D.C. 20559, and request ML-268.

MANDATORY DEPOSIT FOR WORKS PUBLISHED IN THE UNITED STATES WITH NOTICE OF COPYRIGHT

Whether or not copyright registration is sought, the Copyright Act requires that for all works published in the United States bearing a copyright notice, two complete copies of the best edition must be sent to the Copyright Office as a mandatory deposit. It is the responsibility of the owner of copyright or of the exclusive right of distribution to fulfill this mandatory deposit requirement within 3 months after the date of publication in the United States. Failure to make the deposit can result in fines and other penalties, but does not affect copyright protection.

The Copyright Office has issued regulations exempting certain categories of works entirely from the mandatory deposit requirements, and reducing the obligation for certain other categories.

EFFECTIVE DATE OF REGISTRATION

Copyright registration is effective on the date of receipt in the Copyright Office of all the required elements in acceptable form, regardless of the length of time it takes thereafter to process the application and mail the certificate of registration. The length of time required by the Copyright Office to process an application varies from time to time, depending on the amount of material received and the personnel available to handle it. It must also be kept in mind that it may take a number of days for mailed material to reach the Copyright Office and for the certificate of registration to reach the recipient after being mailed by the Copyright Office.

If you are filing an application for copyright registration in the Copyright Office, you *will not* receive an acknowledgement that your application has been received (the Office receives more than 500,000 applications annually), but you can expect:

- A letter or telephone call from a copyright examiner if further information is needed; and
- A certificate of registration to indicate the work has been registered, or if the application cannot be accepted, a letter explaining why it has been rejected.

You may not receive either of these until 90 days have passed.

If you want to know when the Copyright Office receives your material, you should send it via registered or certified mail and request a return receipt.

Notes

CHAPTER 1. FUNDAMENTALS OF COPYRIGHT LAW IN THE UNITED STATES

1. "The Congress shall have the Power . . . To promote the progress of science and useful arts, by securing for limited times to authors and inventors the exclusive right to their respective writings and discoveries. . . ." U.S. Const., art 1, § 8.

2. The first federal copyright statute took effect on May 31, 1790. The present federal copyright statute, the Copyright Revision Act of 1976, Public Law 94-553 (90 Stat. 2541), was signed into law on October 19, 1976, and became effective on January 1, 1978. The official United States Code citation to the Act is 17 U.S.C. § 101 *et seq.* (1976). Unless stated otherwise, all references in the text to the Copyright Act or to the Act are to the 1976 Act.

3. The Register of Copyrights (who directs the Copyright Office) is authorized to establish regulations implementing the functions and duties of the Register under the provision of the Copyright Act (17 U.S.C. § 702). Proposed regulations are reported in the *Federal Register* (published daily by the federal government) when the Copyright Office first gives notice that the regulations are being considered for adoption. A period of time is allowed for the public to make comments about the proposed regulations. If they are adopted, the final version of the regulations is again published in the *Federal Register.* All of the final regulations issued by the Copyright Office are collected in volume 37 of another federal publication, the *Code of Federal Regulations* (cited as 37 *C.F.R.*). Examples of the subject matters covered by the regulations include: registration of claims to copyrights—deposit requirements (37 *C.F.R.* §§ 202.19 and 202.20); methods of affixation and positions of the copyright notice (37 *C.F.R.* § 201.20); and renewal of copyright (37 *C.F.R.* § 202.17).

4. *See* note 2, *supra.*

5. While there is no comprehensive international copyright law in the same sense that there is a United States copyright law, each country usually has its own copyright laws protecting works

that qualify for copyright protection in that country. The United States has entered into treaties with many countries which give reciprocal protection to the works copyrighted in each country. Generally, under these treaties each country gives the same protection to foreign works that it gives to its own domestic works. The United States is also a party to the Universal Copyright Convention (UCC) (first effective on September 15, 1955, with a later revision becoming effective on July 10, 1974) and to the Pan-American Convention, which covers the United States and seventeen Latin American countries (effective since 1910). *See* Copyright Office circulars, numbers 38 and 38a.

6. Statute of Anne.

7. 17 U.S.C. § 102(a).

8. *Report of the House of Representatives on the Copyright Law Revision.* No. 94-1476 at 51, 56-57 (1976) [hereinafter *House Report*].

9. 17 U.S.C. §§ 101, 102(a); *House Report* at 52-53.

10. 17 U.S.C. § 101; *House Report* at 52-53. Prior to the effective date of the 1976 Act (January 1, 1978), copyright was governed by three separate bodies of law. These included state common law, state statutory law, and federal statutory law. State common and statutory law protected a copyrightable work from the time of its creation until the time it was published; at the point of publication, federal law took over. *See House Report* at 129-30. Under the new Act, federal copyright protection is effective as of the time the work is created. Prior to the creation (for example, the artist performs the song but does not fix it), state common and statutory law still apply, and the creator must seek remedies for any theft or infringement in the state courts under state law. *See House Report* at 130-33. Because the work had not been fixed prior to the theft or infringement, the burden of proving authorship is more difficult.

11. 17 U.S.C. § 101.

12. Ibid.

13. *House Report* at 52-53.

14. 17 U.S.C. § 102(a); *House Report* at 53-56.

15. Interestingly, musical works are one of the few types of works not defined in Section 101 of the Act. The drafters of the Act felt the phrase "musical work" had a "fairly settled meaning." *See House Report* at 53. Certain artistic creations, however, such as talking blues and some forms of poetry, may give rise to classification problems.

16. 17 U.S.C. § 101. Sound recordings are copyrightable. 17 U.S.C. § 102(a)(7). Note that a sound recording does not include sounds accompanying a motion picture or other audiovisual work, regardless of whether such sounds are embodied in

disks, tapes or other phonorecords. *See* 17 U.S.C. § 101. Such sounds are a part of the copyrighted movie or audiovisual work. *See House Report* at 56. It is also of interest to note that sound recordings were not recognized as copyrightable works until the enactment of Public Law 92-140 in 1971 (the Sound Recording Amendment of 1971), which applied to all sound recordings fixed on or after February 15, 1972.

17. 17 U.S.C. § 101; *House Report* at 53. Note that while copies generally are material objects from which the work can be visually perceived, "copy" is strictly defined to include all objects other than phonorecords from which the work can be perceived, reproduced or communicated, either directly or through use of a machine. Braille transcriptions and computer datacards are examples of copies from which the work is not visually perceivable.

18. 17 U.S.C. § 101.

19. 17 U.S.C. § 102(b); *House Report* at 56-57. *See Copyright Office* circular 31, *Ideas, Plans, Methods or Systems.*

20. *See* circular R 34 published by the Copyright Office and entitled *Copyright Protection Not Available for Names, Titles, or Short Phrases.*

21. 17 U.S.C. § 701(a).

22. 17 U.S.C. § 702.

23. 17 U.S.C. § 704(a).

24. 17 U.S.C. §§ 705(c), 708(a)(11).

25. 17 U.S.C. §§ 706(a), 708(a)(9) and (11).

26. 17 U.S.C. § 707(a) and (b).

27. 17 U.S.C. §§ 705(b), 708(a)(10).

28. 17 U.S.C. § 201(a); *House Report* at 120-21.

29. 17 U.S.C. § 408(a); *House Report* at 152. *See* Copyright Forms PA, SR, TX, VA.

30. 17 U.S.C. § 201(c); *See House Report* at 122-23.

31. The distinction between a collection and a compilation should be noted. *See* 17 U.S.C. §§ 101, 103, and 201(c). A compilation results from the process of selecting, bringing together, organizing, and arranging previously existing material, regardless of whether the individual items in the material have been or could have been subject to copyright. An example would be a discography of the greatest pop hits of the last twenty years. *See House Report* at 57. A collective work is a species of compilation and involves the selection, assembly, and arrangement of a "number of contributions." Unlike most compilations, each of the contributions incorporated into a collective work must itself constitute a "separate and independent" work. *See House Report* at 122. An example would be the songbook discussed in the text accompanying note 32.

32. 17 U.S.C. §§ 201(c), 103(a).

33. 17 U.S.C. § 201(c).

34. 17 U.S.C. §§ 101, 201(a). A work is a joint work if the authors collaborated with each other or if each of the authors prepared his or her contribution with the knowledge and intention that it would be merged with the contribution of other authors as "inseparable and interdependent parts of a unitary whole." The key is the intention at the time the work is done that its component parts be absorbed or combined into an integrated unit. *See House Report* at 120. Remember that with a collective work, the elements of merger and unity are absent.

35. 17 U.S.C. § 201(b); *House Report* at 121. Section 101 defines a "work made for hire." 17 U.S.C. § 101.

36. In defining "a work made for hire" (17 U.S.C. § 101), the law presumes that a specially ordered or commissioned work is only a work for hire if "the parties expressly agree." The categories of specially commissioned or ordered works are when the work is to be used as: (a) a contribution to a collective work; (b) as part of a motion picture or other audiovisual work; (c) as a translator; (d) as a supplementary work; (e) as a compilation; (f) as an instructional text; (g) as a test; (h) as answer material for a test; or (i) as an atlas. 17 U.S.C. § 101.

37. 17 U.S.C. § 201(d); *House Report* at 61; *see* 17 U.S.C. § 106 (list of enumerated rights) and *House Report* at 123 (transfer of ownership).

38. The Act provides certain limitations on these exclusive rights of the copyright owner (set out in 17 U.S.C. §§ 107-18) so that in strictly defined circumstances others may make certain use of the work with no payment obligations or may obtain a compulsory (automatic) license on the payment of a stated amount. These departures from or limitations on the exclusive rights of the copyright owner are discussed in the concluding subsections of chapter 1 of this book.

39. 17 U.S.C. § 106(1). The right to reproduce refers to the right to produce any material object in which the work is duplicated, transcribed, imitated, or simulated in a fixed form from which it can be perceived, reproduced, or otherwise communicated either directly or with the aid of a machine or device. *See House Report* at 61.

40. 17 U.S.C. § 106(2). A derivative work is a work based upon or adopted from one or more pre-existing works, such as a translation, musical arrangement, dramatization, fictionalization, motion picture version sound recording, art reproduction, or any other form in which a work may be recast, transformed, or adopted. *See* 17 U.S.C. § 101; *House Report* at 62.

41. 17 U.S.C. § 106(3). The right to distribute gives the copyright holder the right to control the first public distribution

of an authorized copy or phonorecord of the work, whether by sale, gift, rental, loan, or lease. Note that subsection 109(a) of the Copyright Act (17 U.S.C. § 109), however, states that the copyright owner's rights with respect to a particular copy or phonorecord cease once he or she has parted with ownership of that particular copy or phonorecord. In other words, a person who buys the record album has the right to sell or otherwise dispose of that album to someone else without needing any prior permission of the copyright owner of the sound recording or of the musical composition embodied in the record. *See House Report* at 62, 79-80. Legislation is pending to limit this right in the case of phonorecord rental.

42. 17 U.S.C. § 106(4); *House Report* at 62-64. To perform a work means to recite, render, play, dance, or act it, either directly or by means of any device or process or, in the case of a motion picture or any other audio-visual work, to show its images in any sequence or to make the accompanying sounds audible. 17 U.S.C. § 101 (defining "perform").

43. 17 U.S.C. § 106(5); *House Report* at 63-64. To display a work means to show a copy of it, either directly or by means of a film, slide, television image, or any other device or process. *See* 17 U.S.C. § 101 (defining "display").

44. *House Report* at 123.

45. "Fair use" was a judicially created doctrine (*House Report* at 65) that has been codified by a legislative directive set forth in § 107. The "not for profit" limitation was implicit in the 1909 Act, as the copyright owner's exclusive right to perform was limited to public performance "for profit" (17 U.S.C. § 101[c], [e] [1909]). Also, the 1909 Act set out a specific exclusion for non-profit educational or charitable performances (17 U.S.C. § 104 [1909]). The Revision Act recodified the "not for profit" limitation in § 110 (17 U.S.C. § 101 [1976]). *See House Report* at 81.

46. 17 U.S.C. § 107. *See generally House Report* at 65-74.

47. 17 U.S.C. § 107(1)-(4).

48. Reproduction of music for classroom use is covered in detail in the *House Report* at 66-72. Copying for performance is prohibited. *See House Report* at 71.

49. 17 U.S.C. § 110; *See generally House Report* at 81-88.

50. A summary of the sanctioned uses includes: (1) a performance or a display of a work by an instructor or pupils in the course of a face-to-face teaching situation in a nonprofit educational institution; (2) the performance of a nondramatic literary or musical work or the display of that work in the course of a transmission when (a) the performance or display is a regular part of the systematic, instructional activities of a nonprofit edu-

cational institution or a governmental body, (b) the performance or display is directly related and of material assistance to the teaching effort, and (c) the transmission is made primarily (i) for reception in classrooms or similar places of instruction, or (ii) for reception by persons to whom the transmission is directed because of disability or who for other reasons are not able to attend a classroom (*see* 27 *C.F.R.* § 201.15 on use for the blind and physically handicapped), or (iii) for reception by officers or employees of governmental bodies as a part of their official duties; (3) the performance of a nondramatic literary or musical work, or of a dramatic-musical work of a religious nature or the display of such work when it occurs in the course of religious services at a place of worship or other religious assembly; and (4) the performance of a nondramatic literary or musical work without any direct or indirect commercial advantage and without the payment of any fee or other compensation to any performers, promoters, or organizers, provided that (a) there is no direct or indirect admission charge or (b) the proceeds of any charge that is made after costs are used exclusively for educational, religious, or charitable purposes and not for private financial gain. With regard to the performance described in subsection (4) of this footnote, the copyright owner or its agent has the right to object to such performance if the procedures set out in 17 U.S.C. § 110(4)(B) of the Act and in the relevant Copyright Office regulations at 37 *C.F.R.* § 201.13 are followed.

51. There also are further limitations on the copyright owner's exclusive rights that are not covered by this book. The reader is directed to the relevant sections of the Copyright Act to study those limitations, namely: (1) reproduction by libraries and archives (17 U.S.C. § 108; *House Report* at 74-79; 37 C.F.R. § 201. 14); (2) effect of transfer of a particular copy of phonorecord (17 U.S.C. § 109; *see* note 41, *supra; House Report* at 79-81); (3) secondary transmissions (17 U.S.C. § 111; *House Report* at 88-101); (4) ephemeral recordings (17 U.S.C. § 112; *House Report* at 101-05); (5) pictorial, graphic, and sculptural works (17 U.S.C. § 113; *House Report* at 105-06); (6) computers and similar information systems (17 U.S.C. § 117; *House Report* at 116); and (7) non-commercial broadcasting (17 U.S.C. § 118; *House Report* at 116-20). The remaining sections of chapter 1 of Title 17—§ 114 (sound recordings), § 115 (compulsory licensing for making and distributing phonorecords), and § 116 (public performances by means of coin-operated phonorecord players)—are discussed in chapter 1 of this book: ("Limitations on Exclusive Rights in Sound Recordings" and "Compulsory Licenses as a Limitation on Exclusive Rights in Musical Works") and chapter 5 ("Juke Box Compulsory License"), respectively.

52. 17 U.S.C. § 115(a)(1).

53. 17 U.S.C. § 115(c)(2).

54. Ibid. A phonorecord is considered distributed when the person exercising the compulsory license has voluntarily and permanently parted with its possession.

55. 17 U.S.C. § 115(a)(1).

56. *House Report* at 108.

57. Under the old law the copyright owner in a musical work was required to file a notice of use on Form U in the Copyright Office as a condition for receiving royalties from anyone who recorded that work without an express license. Since this requirement has been dropped from the new law, the Copyright Office will no longer record notices of use on Form U, and this is true even if the work was originally copyrighted or released on records before January 1, 1978 (the effective date of the new law). *See* Copyright Office circular RS1. Under the new Act, a person making a sound recording under a compulsory license must notify the copyright owner of his or her intent to use the compulsory license within 30 days of the making of the sound recording, and before any distribution of the record (17 U.S.C. § 115[b][1]). If the Copyright Office cannot identify the copyright owner, notice to the Copyright Office itself is sufficient to satisfy the notice requirement (17 U.S.C. § 115[b][1]). The notice under the Act must comply in form, content, and service with the regulations that the Register of Copyrights shall prescribe. Anyone contemplating the use of the compulsory licensing procedures under the Act should submit a written notice to the Copyright Office setting out the identity of the intended uses, the song, and its owner. Failure to notify the copyright owner forecloses the possibility of a compulsory license. Unless the person making the recording negotiates a license with the copyright owner permitting recording of the song, the making and distribution of phonorecord embodying the copyrighted song is an infringement (17 U.S.C. § 115[b][2]).

In order to receive royalty payments under a compulsory license, the copyright owner must be identified in the public records of the Copyright Office. Failing to so identify the copyright owner strips the copyright owner of the right to royalty payments (17 U.S.C. § 115[c][1]). Royalty payments must be made to the copyright owner by the 20th of the month, and must include payments covering all records made and distributed in the immediately preceding month. The compulsory license user also must file an annual report certified by a certified public accountant (17 U.S.C. § 115[c][3]).

If the copyright owner fails to receive either the monthly payment or the monthly and annual account statements, he or she may give written notice to the licensed user that the license automatically will terminate if the default is not corrected within 30 days of the date of notice. If the licensed user fails to correct the default, any making or distribution of records under the terminated license is an infringement (17 U.S.C. § 115[c][4]).

58. 17 U.S.C. § 115(a)(2); *see generally House Report* at 107-11; *see* interim regulations at 42 Fed. Reg. 64889-94 (December 29, 1978). This requirement is imposed so the work is not "perverted, distorted, or travestied" (*House Report* at 109). While interpretation of a song is allowed, it is unclear just how far an artist may go in changing the song. It would seem, however, that an artist or writer receiving royalties under the compulsory license is unlikely to sue under this provision, unless he or she deems the musical integrity of the work to outweigh the royalties being generated under the license.

59. 17 U.S.C. § 115(a)(2).

60. 17 U.S.C. § 114(a) and (b); *House Report* at 106-07.

61. 17 U.S.C. § 114(c).

62. *See* note 60, *supra*. See discussion in chapter 4 of this book concerning commercial exploitation of songs and sound recordings.

63. Recently, the Copyright Office has taken the position that performers and record producers should enjoy rights with respect to public performances of sound recordings to which they have contributed (Copyright Announcement ML-197, p. 3, 42 *Federal Register* No. 59, pp. 12763-8). The most likely approach would be a form of compulsory license, and a bill providing for such was pending in the 95th Congress, HR 6063, 95th Congress, 1st Sess. 1977. The Copyright Office has proposed a revised version of this bill.

CHAPTER 2. OBTAINING A COPYRIGHT

1. 17 U.S.C. § 401(b).

2. Ibid.

3. The use of the symbol © is prescribed by the Universal Copyright Convention (the UCC), an international treaty to which the United States is a party. The UCC, as drafted in Geneva in 1952, came into force on September 16, 1955, and as revised at Paris in 1971 came into force on July 10, 1974. While there is no such thing as an international copyright that will automatically protect an author's writing throughout the world, as a general rule the UCC requires a participating country to give the

same protection to foreign works that meet the UCC requirements as it gives to its own domestic works. Current United States copyright relations with the nations of the world are listed in the Copyright Office circular R 38a, *International Copyright Relations of the United States*, available free of charge from the Copyright Office.

4. If you want to use both the word "copyright" and the symbol ©, make sure you put them in the order. "Copyright © 1978," rather than "© Copyright 1978," as the UCC requires that the © accompany the date and the copyright owner's name.

5. 17 U.S.C. § 402(b). The symbol P also has been adopted as the international symbol for protection of sound recordings by the Phonograms Convention. (The Convention for the Protection of Producers of Phonograms Against Unauthorized Duplication of Their Phonograms, done at Geneva, October 29, 1971), to which the United States is a party effective March 10, 1974.

6. 17 U.S.C. § 401(b)(2). The year to be used in the copyright notice illustrates another interesting distinction made in the Act. The period of copyright protection (life of the author plus fifty years), runs as of the year in which the work is created. *See* 17 U.S.C. § 302(a). The year to be inserted in the notice, however, is the year work is first *published*. *See* 17 U.S.C. § 401(b)(2). So, if a song created (fixed) in 1978 is not published until 1980, then the year to be inserted in the notice is 1980 and not 1978.

Copyright protection and duration under the prior law began as of the date of publication rather than creation (17 U.S.C. § 24 [1952]) so that a work created (fixed) in 1958 but not published until 1960 would not have been covered by the federal copyright law until 1960, which also would have been the year in the copyright notice. Thus, the date in that notice would have been given an accurate reading of the work's copyright year.

7. Western Hemisphere copyright relations are partially governed by a series of seven Pan-American Copyright Conventions. The most important of these is the Buenos Aires Convention of 1910, which the United States and seventeen Latin American nations have ratified. It specifies that authors of any contracting country who have secured copyrights in their own country will enjoy in each of the other countries the rights it accords its own work, if the work contains "a statement indicating the reservation of the property rights."

The words "All rights reserved" therefore denote the reservation of copyright in the Western Hemisphere countries that have ratified the Buenos Aires Convention of 1910. Such words are not required by United States copyright law, have no effect as far as the United States law is concerned, and should not be considered a substitute for the formal notice requirement prescribed by United States copyright law. They should be used in addition to the copyright notice required by the Act.

8. 17 U.S.C. § 401(a); *House Report* at 145.

9. 17 U.S.C. § 402(c).

10. Telephone conversation by J. Gunnar Erickson on July 19, 1978, with Information Officer of U.S. Copyright Office.

11. Act of October 15, 1971 (Pub. Law 92-140, 85 Stat. 391), as further amended by the Act of December 31, 1974 (Pub. Law 93-573, 88 Stat. 1873).

12. 17 U.S.C. § 101.

13. 17 U.S.C. § 401(b)(2).

14. 17 U.S.C. §§ 405, 406.

15. 17 U.S.C. § 405(a)(1)-(3).

16. 17 U.S.C. § 405(b).

17. 17 U.S.C. § 408(a).

18. 17 U.S.C. § 408(b). The regulations governing deposit requirements appeared at 43 F.R. 763 (January 4, 1978) and will form 37 *C.F.R.* 202. Generally, disk is preferred to tape and open reel to cassette.

19. 17 U.S.C. §§ 101, 102.

20. *See* instructions to Form SR in the Appendix.

21. 17 U.S.C. § 408(c)(1) states in part: "This administrative classification of works has no significance with respect to the subject matter of copyright or the exclusive rights provided by this title."

22. 17 U.S.C. § 708(a).

23. *See* note 22, *supra.*

24. 17 U.S.C. § 407(a)1 *but see* 17 U.S.C. § 407(c) (copyright regulations may be exempt or reduce deposit requirements).

25. 17 U.S.C. § 407(d)(1), (2).

26. 17 U.S.C. § 407(d)(3).

27. 17 U.S.C. § 408(b).

CHAPTER 3. DURATION AND TRANSFER OF THE COPYRIGHT

1. 17 U.S.C. § 24 (1909).

2. 17 U.S.C. § 302(a); *House Report* at 133-36. The term of all such copyrights run until the end of the calendar year of the expiration year. *See* 17 U.S.C. § 305.

3. For works created before January 1, 1978, but which as of that date are not published or are registered in unpublished

form, the duration of the copyright will be governed by 17 U.S.C. § 302 (i.e., the work will be treated as though it were created on or after January 1, 1978). *See* 17 U.S.C. § 303.

4. 17 U.S.C. § 302(b); *House Report* at 136-37.

5. 17 U.S.C. § 302(c); *House Report* at 137-38. *See* 17 U.S.C. § 302(d) and (e) and *House Report* at 138 on records and presumptions of an author's death, which present practical answers to the problem of discovering death dates of obscure or unknown authors.

6. 17 U.S.C. § 302(c).

7. 17 U.S.C. § 304(a); *House Report* at 139.

8. 17 U.S.C. § 304(b); *see* 43 Fed. Reg. 964-65 (January 5, 1978).

9. 17 U.S.C. § 201(d)(1); *House Report* at 123.

10. 17 U.S.C. § 202; *House Report* at 124.

11. 17 U.S.C. § 204(a) and § 205(a).

12. 17 U.S.C. § 204(a); *House Report* at 128-29; 43 Fed. Reg. 771-74 (January 4, 1978). After filing the document of transfer, the Register of Copyrights will record the document and return a certificate of recordation. 17 U.S.C. § 205(b). Recording the transfer document gives all persons constructive notice of the facts in that document if it identifies the transferred work and the work itself has been registered. *See* 17 U.S.C. § 205(c).

13. 17 U.S.C. § 205(d).

14. Ibid.

15. 17 U.S.C. § 205(e).

16. 17 U.S.C. § 203; *House Report* at 124-28.

17. 17 U.S.C. § 24 (1909).

18. *See generally* 17 U.S.C. § 28 (1909) [assignability of copyrights]. This assumes, of course, that there were no contractual terms providing for return of the assigned rights.

19. 17 U.S.C. § 24 (1909).

20. 17 U.S.C. § 304(c).

21. 17 U.S.C. § 304(c)(3).

22. 17 U.S.C. § 304(c)(4)(A).

23. 17 U.S.C. § 203(a)(3); *see House Report* at 126, and examples therein. Termination of grants involving joint works and deceased authors are provided for in 17 U.S.C. § 203(a)(1) and (2) and § 304(c); *see House Report* at 125-26.

24. 17 U.S.C. § 203(a)(3).

25. 17 U.S.C. § 203(a)(4).

26. 17 U.S.C. § 203(a)(4)(A).

27. 17 U.S.C. § 203(b).

28. 17 U.S.C. § 203(b)(6).

29. 17 U.S.C. § 203(b)(4).

30. 17 U.S.C. § 203(b)(1).

CHAPTER 4. INCOME FROM MUSIC

1. 17 U.S.C. § 115(c).
2. 17 U.S.C. § 115(c).
3. 17 U.S.C. § 106(4).
4. M. Ashburne, *Black Music: A Financial Perspective* (1977) at 267.
5. 17 U.S.C. § 106(3).
6. M. Tolleson, "The Music Business: Who Pays the Piper," *The Texas Observer*, April 14, 1978, at 5.
7. 17 U.S.C. § 114(a).
8. 17 U.S.C. § 114(d) requires the Register of Copyrights to submit recommendations to Congress on whether the Act should be amended to provide for performance rights in sound recordings. The addenda to the Register's report on this issue contained an economic analysis of the impact of allowing a royalty on the performance of a sound recording and generally endorsed such a requirement. 43 Federal Register 11773 (March 21, 1978). *See* note 63 to chapter 1.
9. 17 U.S.C. § 201(b). *See* also chapter 1.
10. Synchronization is a form of reproduction of the copyrighted musical work; exhibition of the film is a performance of that copyrighted musical work. These are the distinct and exclusive rights: 17 U.S.C. § 106(1) [reproduction] and 17 U.S.C. § 106(4) [public performance].
11. 17 U.S.C. § 101; *House Report* at 56.

CHAPTER 5. INFRINGEMENT

1. *House Report* at 158.
2. The exclusive rights in copyright are set out in 17 U.S.C. §§ 106-18. They are discussed in chapter 1, *supra*.
3. 17 U.S.C. § 501(a). Importation of copies or phonorecords as an infringement is set out in 17 U.S.C. § 602. *See House Report* at 169-71.
4. *House Report* at 61.
5. It is difficult to envision an infringement suit based on violation of right to display a musical work; there is also a paucity of legislative guidance. *See House Report* at 64-65.
6. *House Report* at 106.
7. Ibid.

8. Compulsory and negotiated mechanical licenses are discussed in chapter 1 of this book. The important distinction here is that under a license, performers are free to imitate the sound recording as closely as possible; however, there is no right (nor a compulsory license) to simply remix the actual sound of the original sound recording. An interesting example of a remix is Debbie Boone's hit-making rendition of "You Light Up My Life." The song also won an Academy Award. Boone's rendition, however, was not the version in the movie. The rendition was recorded after the release of the movie *You Light Up My Life*. The same sound track was used, except Boone's voice was substituted for the original singer's.

9. *See* discussion of fair use in chapter 1 of this book.

10. *Krofft Television Productions, Inc.* v. *McDonald's Corp.*, 562 F.2d 1157 (9th Cir. 1977); *Nimmer on Copyright*, Section 141.2 at 610-11 (1976).

11. Krofft, ibid., *Nimmer* Section 141.2 at 613.

12. *See Bright Tunes Music Corp.* v. *Harrisongs Music Ltd.*, 420 F. Supp. 177, 180-81 (S.D.N.Y. 1976 [hereinafter "Bright Tunes"].

13. Bright Tunes, *supra.* at 181.

14. 420 F. Supp. 177 at 179.

15. Not only did Harrison testify that the songs were substantially similar, but the "Belmonts" recorded a later version of "My Sweet Lord" in which they interlayed the words of both "He's So Fine" and "My Sweet Lord." 420 F. Supp. 177 at 181, footnote 13. The similarity, then, was apparent to persons outside the courtroom as well.

16. 420 F. Supp. 177 at 180.

17. 17 U.S.C. § 501(b).

18. 17 U.S.C. §§ 408, 412.

19. 17 U.S.C. §§ 502 and 504(b).

20. 17 U.S.C. 412(1). Statutory damages are discussed *infra*.

21. 17 U.S.C. 412(2).

22. 17 U.S.C. 412(1).

23. These methods include repressing, transcribing, or recapturing off the air. *See House Report* at 106. Thus, if an FM station plays an album that you record on tape at home, and you then sell copies of the tape, you are infringing the sound recording even though you did not tape the sound recording directly from the phonorecord. This exemplifies the most typical infringement of sound recordings, that is, by sale of unauthorized tapes.

24. *House Report* at 106.

25. Ibid.

26. *See* chapter 1 of this book.

27. The present rate, as discussed earlier, is either 4½ cents per song, or .85 cents per minute of playing time, whichever is larger.

28. *See, e.g.,* California Business and Professsions Code 17500.

29. *See* chapter 1 of this book.

30. Again, the distinction between the underlying musical works and the sounds embodied in the sound recording is crucial here. Once a song (musical work) is recorded, you are free, within the compulsory license provisions, to re-record the song, but not to appropriate the actual sounds form the sound recording. You must create your own version.

31. 17 U.S.C. § 106(1); *House Report* at 108 and cases cited therein.

32. 17 U.S.C. §§ 502, 603.

33. *House Report* at 160.

34. Injunctions to prevent infringing importation are unique in that they prohibit infringement before it happens. Typically, though, an injunction issues to revent further infringement. An injunction prohibiting a domestic infringement before it occurs would likely constitute an invalid prior restraint. *See Nebraska Press Ass'n.* v. *Stuart* 427 U.S. 539 (1976).

35. 17 U.S.C. § 502(b); *House Report* at 160.

36. 17 U.S.C. § 503(a); *House Report* at 160.

37. Although from the language of the Act it appears a record pressing machine used to make infringing phonorecords might be ordered destroyed by the court, this is highly unlikely. The record pressing machine likely is also used for non-infringing reproduction. For a discussion of this, *see Nimmer on Copyright.* Section 158-19.

38. *House Report* at 160.

39. 17 U.S.C. § 504(c).

40. The law makes it easier to prove profits by providing that the infringement victim only prove the infringer's gross revenue. *See* 17 U.S.C. § 504(b). After this is done, the infringer may reduce this amount by proving deductible expenses and elements of profit attributable to factors other than infringing the copyrighted work.

41. 17 U.S.C. §§ 504(a)(1) and 504(b).

42. Recovery under 17 U.S.C. §§ 504(a) or 504(b) is stated in the alternative.

43. 17 U.S.C. § 504(c)(1).

44. Ibid. Also *House Report* at 162.

45. *House Report* at 162.

46. Ibid.

47. Ibid.
48. 17 U.S.C. § 504(c)(1).
49. 17 U.S.C. § 504(c)(2).
50. The burden of proof to show "willfullness" is on the copyright owner; the burden to show innocent infringement is on the infringer. *House Report* at 162-3; 17 U.S.C. § 504(c)(2).
51. 17 U.S.C. § 504(c)(2).
52. Ibid. Also *House Report* at 163.
53. 17 U.S.C § 505.
54. *See Nimmer on Copyright*, Section 161 at 705.
55. 17 U.S.C. § 505(a).
56. Ibid. The same special penalties apply to infringers of motion pictures.
57. Ibid.
58. 17 U.S.C. §§ 505(b) and 509. *See* discussion in note 37, *supra.*
59. 17 U.S.C. § 506(c).
60. 17 U.S.C. § 506(d).
61. 17 U.S.C. § 506(e).
62. 17 U.S.C. § 507(a) and (b).
63. 17 U.S.C. § 116.
64. 17 U.S.C. § 116(b)(1)(A).
65. 17 U.S.C. § 116(b)(1)(C).
66. The infringement (17 U.S.C. § 116(a)) is playing the phonorecords on a juke box without the compulsory license, which violates the copyright owner's exclusive right to perform set out in 17 U.S.C. § 106(4). Again, only the owner of the copyright in the underlying song and not the person making the sound recording embodied in the phonorecord, may sue.
67. 17 U.S.C. § 116(d).
68. 17 U.S.C. § 116(c)(2).
69. 17 U.S.C. § 116(c)(4)(B).
70. 17 U.S.C. §§ 602-603.
71. 17 U.S.C. § 602(b).
72. 17 U.S.C. § 602(a).
73. *House Report* at 169-71.
74. *See* the execptions: government importation (602(a)(1)); private use (602(a)(2) discussed *infra*); and scholarly, educational, or religious organizations or purpose (602(a)(3)).
75. 17 U.S.C. § 602(a)(2).
76. Ibid. Also *House Report* at 170.
77. 17 U.S.C. § 602(b).
78. 17 U.S.C. § 603. A person seeking exclusion may get an injunction prohibiting importation, but may be required to post a surety bond to cover any damage caused by an unjustified exclusion. *See* 17 U.S.C. § 603(b)(2).

79. 17 U.S.C. § 603(c).
80. Discussed in chapter 1 of this book.
81. 17 U.S.C. § 106(2).
82. 17 U.S.C. § 101.
83. This is the so-called audience test. *See generally Nimmer on Copyright* §§ 143.5-143.53, pp. 634-43. The recent Krofft case labels this test as an "intrinsic test" (562 F.2d 1157 at 1164-65). It depends on the response of the "ordinary reasonable person."
84. 17 U.S.C. §§ 101 and 103.
85. 17 U.S.C. § 103(b).
86. Ibid.
87. 17 U.S.C. 107. *See generally Nimmer on Copyright* § 145, pp. 643-56.
88. *Nimmer on Copyright*, § 145, p. 646. These criteria are embodied in 17 U.S.C § 107(4).
89. This assumes that the work is a phonorecord being used commercially.
90. For an excellent discussion of this concept, *see Nimmer on Copyright* § 145, pp. 646-49.

Index